Industrial Jobs and the Worker

Industrial Jobs and the Worker

*An Investigation of Response
to Task Attributes*

ARTHUR N. TURNER   AND   PAUL R. LAWRENCE
Associate Professor of   *Professor of*
Business Administration   *Organizational Behavior*

HARVARD UNIVERSITY · DIVISION OF RESEARCH
GRADUATE SCHOOL OF BUSINESS ADMINISTRATION
Boston 1965

Library of Congress Catalog Card No. 64–7523

Printed in the United States of America

Foreword

Research into what is usually called the intrinsic job has an honorable ancestry, stretching from the work of the British Medical Council during and after World War I, the early work of Mayo, on through research of the Tavistock Institute in England, of the Centre des Arts et Metiers and other groups in France, and of the Technology Project at Yale University. More recently there have been important studies in the field at Michigan, Berkeley, Chicago, and elsewhere. The authors of this book build solidly on both the conceptual and the empirical contributions from these sources and from many others. But with methodological tools, improved and tailored to fit the contemporary scene, they have adopted a new approach. Essentially their end-product is a new instrument for applied research, of equal interest to the student and to the administrator concerned with machine-related work problems in the modern world.

Thanks to lucid exposition the problem addressed by the authors can be expressed very simply and sharply. "Our purpose," they write, "was to develop and implement a method of measuring job attributes that would help predict workers' response to their jobs across a wide range of differing technologies."

There are no redundant words in this compressed statement, which in a sense sums up and comprehends both their research design and a *purpose* carried out over three years of research. The authors did develop a *method* of *measuring* job attributes, calling it a "Requisite Task Attributes Index," RTA for short. They *implemented* their measuring method in a varied sample of industrial jobs drawn from eleven industries. They *predicted workers' response,* both subjective and behavioral, across *differing technologies.* How their research trail led them sometimes across sterile ground, but more often to pay dirt, is the substance and for the reader the excitement of this book.

Another short passage from the first chapter is even more useful in underscoring the book's aim, and the authors' basic hypotheses. ". . . this research started with the concept that every industrial job contained certain technologically determined task attributes which would influence workers' response. By 'task attributes' we meant such characteristics of the job as the amount of variety, autonomy, responsibility, and interaction with others built into its design." This passage defines clearly the research area the authors have chosen, as well as suggesting something of its broader social significance. The key lies in the phrase "technologically determined." Until recently the bulk of research on work and the worker has been focused upon nontechnological factors such as styles of supervision, union influence, wage systems, and so forth. Indeed, until a decade ago most efforts to solve work problems at the factory level took little account of "differing technologies." It had been commonly assumed by both theorists and practitioners that the technology conditioning a job was an immutable "given." Turner and Lawrence firmly challenge this assumption.

The words "workers' response" can be usefully expanded. Evidence from this and other recent research shows that "response" is a spectrum stretching from mild satisfaction to enthusiastic involvement in one's work; and negatively from mild dissatisfaction to obsessive dislike, behaviorally expressed in absenteeism, turnover, sabotage, or the strike. A better understanding of "response" and its social implications as used in this research report emerges when one considers the nature of the job attributes considered, "autonomy, responsibility, interaction with others," etc. Notice that the authors are here stating their initial assumption that these socially significant aspects of human work are in considerable degree "technologically determined" and also that they have been built into the job design. The phrase "built into" suggests that somebody has built them in. Indeed the last chapter of the book contains many practical hints for the architects of new industrial jobs in the future, as well as for the redesign of existing jobs which are causing work problems.

But to go back to the trail of research followed here. Implicit in these brief introductory sentences are the major hypotheses which the authors set out to test. There were two of them. In each the sums of the attributes of each job studied, and expressed in the RTA Index, were taken as independent variables. On the other hand, the workers' responses, measured mainly, though not wholly, by an index of high or low attendance at work, and by subjective expressions of satisfaction, were the dependent variables.

In greatly oversimplified form then, the two major hypotheses were these:

That job satisfaction will be high on high RTA Index jobs, i.e., jobs that are high on autonomy, responsibility, interaction opportunities, etc., whereas satisfaction will be low on low RTA Index jobs. That there will be high attendance (low absenteeism) when RTA Index scores are high, and low attendance on low RTA jobs.

Generally speaking, these two major hypotheses were validated, a certain ambiguity, however, appearing in the "satisfaction" finding. The ambiguity fortunately led the authors into a wholly new research path which yielded useful and unexpected results. Before turning to those results it is important to ask: What about the other factors and features of work life, supervision, the union, wages, personality traits, and other topics which previous research had tended to highlight? Did they have no effect, or did Turner and Lawrence ignore them? They had their effects, of course, and they were fully considered by the investigators as "supplementary variables." In fact the precise way in which each of them did or did not have substantial bearing on the other detailed findings presented is an incisive and satisfactory section of the book. The most important and definitive finding, however, is that for the total population studied — no matter what the effect of intervening variables in influencing response variables in individual cases — technologically job-determined attributes dominated worker response. This was true whether that response was positive or negative.

It remains of course for future research to broaden the application of this or some other RTA Index to a wider span of technologies and especially to those which will be increasingly influenced by the computer or other forms of automation. Only then will we begin to know in all its dimensions the impact of science and technology on human work.

A promising start toward much deeper and wider exploration was taken by these authors almost by accident. As mentioned above, in analyzing the data validating one of their major hypotheses, the authors were puzzled by an ambiguity, which fortunately led to the discovery that they had neglected an important "supplementary variable," subcultural influence. When their hypotheses were applied to two cultural subgroups in their total population, their findings were modified in a fashion to open up several useful and challenging questions. The two subcultural groups were workers in rural or town surroundings, and workers in urban or city environments. The authors called the subgroups, for short, "Town" and "City." Focusing on the Town and City subgroups this is what the investigators found:

It was true that a positive correlation existed between high RTA jobs and attendance of the population as a whole, but the correlation turned out to be far higher for the Town than for the City group. And the over-all hypothesis of greater satisfaction with high RTA jobs was confirmed only for Town workers, not for the population as a whole. Further, when the satisfaction hypothesis was applied to the City group only, the correlation proved negative. It is worth making perfectly clear what this finding is and what it is not. In doing so, we shall be helped by a shorthand expression the investigators adopted in their later chapters. They called jobs with high RTA indices examples of "complex" work; jobs with low RTA indices examples of "simple" work. Adopting then this simplified terminology, the modified finding seemed to say this: Town or rural workers tend to react positively to more complex work, i.e., work requiring the exercise of greater skill and the acceptance of more responsibility. On the other hand, City workers tended to react negatively to this kind of work but positively to simpler tasks requiring the exercise of less skill and the acceptance of less responsibility.

It is important to notice two things about this modified finding: First it does not affect the general finding that very important correlation exists between technologically determined job characteristics and worker response. But second it poses challenging questions of broad social significance. Perhaps the most obvious of these is this: What is the changing nature of work doing to our cultural values? Fortunately the final two chapters which analyze this modified finding and explore both its administrative and social significance are a rewarding climax to the book.

Nor do the authors neglect the very practical question, what to do *now* about machine-related problems in both Town and City work groups. The final chapter is rich in suggestions for managers assigned the responsibility of designing or redesigning jobs to meet practical problems.

New technologies are appearing with breathtaking rapidity, and the old molds into which work content were poured for many years are being broken down. This would appear then to be a time for imaginative architects of a new world of work. If that be true, this is the book for them.

CHARLES R. WALKER

Boston, Massachusetts
October 1964

The financial support for this study came in part from an allocation of funds contributed by The Associates of the Harvard Business School and in part from an allocation of a grant to the School by the Ford Foundation for research in the field of organizational behavior. I express for all at the School our gratitude for this generous support of our research activities.

BERTRAND FOX
Director of Research

Soldiers Field
Boston, Massachusetts
October 1964

Acknowledgments

MANY PERSONS have given the authors valuable help in the course of this study. Clearly our work would have been impossible without the cooperation of members of the organizations within which the field work was conducted — the managers who generously agreed to let us use their organizations as our research sites, the supervisors who kindly accepted our interruptions and were responsive to our many questions, the workmen who with tolerance and good nature let us observe them perform their jobs and who thoughtfully answered our lengthy questionnaire. Many of these people believed that in some way this study would help them, and we hope that, in the long run, it will.

It is difficult to specify from which authors and colleagues came many ideas and concepts which, sometimes in circuitous fashion, found their way into the design and implementation of the research, and into the manner in which we have interpreted our findings. Those of whom we are most aware can be found in the bibliography and in the references to other studies we have given in the text, especially in Chapter 1.

For their interest and encouragement we are especially grateful to two long-time friends, associates, and teachers: Fritz J. Roethlisberger, Wallace Brett Donham Professor of Human Relations at the Harvard Business School, and Charles R. Walker, formerly Director of Research, the Technology Project, Institute of Human Relations, Yale University. We have learned much from them about research and writing.

Other colleagues who have influenced us in the present study include Robert Guest, Professor of Administration at the Amos Tuck School of Business Administration, Dartmouth College, and Eric Trist, Kenneth Rice, and their co-workers at the Tavistock Institute of Human Relations, London. In particular we received useful and specific suggestions for improving the manuscript from Professors Edmund P. Learned, Lewis B. Ward, and Abraham Zaleznik of the Harvard Business School, as well as from Professor Bertrand Fox, our Director of Research.

In addition, we received skillful and valuable assistance in collecting and analyzing the data from Laurent Picard and Peter Vaill, now faculty members of the University of Montreal and the University of California at Los Angeles, respectively, and from Andrew Priem, doctoral candidate at the Harvard Business School. Mrs. Bertha Daniels of the Data Processing Bureau at the School, and Miss Ruth Norton, Editor and Executive Secretary of the Division of Research, each generously contributed her unique skill to our efforts with patience and humor. The typing of many drafts and numerous other data handling jobs were ably and cheerfully performed by Mrs. Charlotte Welsh, Miss Susan Muldoon, Mrs. Marie Bishop, and Mrs. Nina Frank. Miss Lorna Daniells of Baker Library helped with the bibliography, and Mrs. Anne Cronin drew the charts.

Finally our wives, Nancy and Martha, in this as in many other things, have helped us most of all.

We alone are responsible for the faults that remain in this study in spite of all this help.

ARTHUR N. TURNER

PAUL R. LAWRENCE

Soldiers Field
Boston, Massachusetts
October 1964

Contents

List of Exhibits

Industrial Jobs and the Worker

CHAPTER 1

Background and Design of the Study

IN AN ERA of advanced and rapidly advancing technology, many researchers and social commentators have drawn attention to the impact of technology on human behavior and attitudes. Studies of the relationship between "man and the machine" are concerned with a wide variety of aspects of this problem.[1] Technology has important impacts on human behavior that have been studied and need to be understood in terms of the larger society, the industry, the enterprise, the smaller group within an organization, and the individual worker. And at each "level," in this sense, the impacts of technology have been and need to be studied from different points of view, making use of a number of different intellectual disciplines. The research to be described here belongs within this broad field of concern.

Many writers on the general topic apparently assume as given that modern technology condemns the majority of the industrial work force to a routine and unchallenging life at work, and turn their attention to ways in which this might be counteracted through more meaningful leisure activities.[2] Many businessmen also assume that this condition can best be cured by providing antidotes and palliatives, as illustrated by the comments elicited in a 1948 survey on the "problem of boredom" by the National Industrial Conference Board.

[1] Examples of statements of general concern with this problem are given in Walker (1962) and in the writings of authors such as Bell (1956), Ohmann (1955), Swados (1959), and Friedmann (1955, 1956, 1961). A useful summary of research on "Technology and Job Satisfaction" is provided by Strauss and Sayles (1960). A significant study by Blauner (1964) has appeared as we go to press.

[2] See, for example, Riesman and Bloomberg (1957) and Levenstein (1962).

1

The present research attempts to test the validity of both these assumptions.

The particular focus of this study is on the response of workers to variations in the nature of work that are to a large extent technologically determined. How do industrial workers respond to various characteristics of the intrinsic job? What is their reaction to the actual physical and mental operations inherent in the design of their jobs, or what in this study we have termed the "attributes" or "technologically determined characteristics" of the task? More specifically, our study was designed to make a unique contribution in the following respects:

1. To develop a scheme for classifying relevant task attributes, and a methodology for measuring them quantitatively across a wide range of technologies and types of work.
2. To formulate and test a general hypothesis that workers would express a more favorable response to more complex or involving tasks than to more highly programmed, less demanding work.
3. To account for results inconsistent with the above hypothesis; for example, by examining response to the nature of work by various subpopulations of workers included in the total sample studied.

Implicit to our research objectives was the idea that workers' response to task attributes could and should become a more important factor in job design. We believed that a necessary first step in this direction would be to study response to the task across a relatively wide range of technological settings. We hoped that our methods and findings would eventually be useful to managers responsible for the design of industrial jobs.

Research on worker behavior in organizations has tended increasingly, over the last twenty or thirty years, to stress social structure at work, leadership styles, interpersonal relationships, and, more recently perhaps, individual predispositions and personality factors. Since we are not attempting to deny or ignore the importance of these variables, a review seems appropriate concerning the place of our present line of research within this larger context.

In 1923 Elton Mayo conducted a field study of response to repetitive work in the mule spinning department of a textile mill, which he summarized ten years later in Chapter 2 of *The Human Problems of an Industrial Civilization*.[3] This study called attention to the importance of the motor and mental requisites inherent in a particular job design, and related them to psychological and social factors influencing worker behavior. In a similar manner, several of the studies conducted in the 1920's and 1930's by the British Industrial Fatigue Research Board (later called the Industrial Health Research Board) combined detailed attention to the minutiae of a particular job design with due recognition of the larger social-psychological context within which a given job was performed.[4] Thus from the earliest days of systematic behavioral research in industry, both job attributes and social-psychological factors were considered relevant, and in all the more pertinent studies since then of behavior within organizations, in our opinion, it has never been a question of exclusively choosing one emphasis at the expense of the other.

As is well known, the Western Electric studies did produce a powerful and justified trend in favor of social and interpersonal considerations and away from those that were solely economic and physiological.[5] Started by the company itself as an investigation of the consequences of changes in the intensity of artificial lighting, the research at Hawthorne grew into a comprehensive investigation of social structure at the work group level, with important implications for administrative

[3] Mayo (1933; 1946), pp. 43–54.
[4] See listings in Bibliography under Great Britain Industrial Health (Fatigue) Research Board.
[5] Roethlisberger and Dickson (1939).

behavior. But we believe that some of the interpretation of the Western Electric research as downgrading the relative impact of job attributes on behavior has been mistaken. The Western Electric studies and subsequent research belonging to the same tradition have certainly demonstrated that social and interpersonal factors are more relevant in understanding worker behavior than many of the economic and technical "logics" which have usually been relied upon by those responsible for designing jobs and conditions of work. In fact, this finding has been rediscovered so frequently that there should be little need to reiterate it.

Yet this does not mean that economic and technological variables are irrelevant; rather, it means that we need more adequate schemes for taking them into account. For example, workers do not respond to monetary incentives solely in terms of their individual economic self-interest. Nevertheless, the economic aspects of motivation remain highly relevant. Money is still important, but often in ways that contradict the assumptions underlying the design of traditional individual piece-work systems.[6]

In a similar fashion, our research starts with the belief that technology and job design are still important determinants of worker response, but perhaps in ways that frequently contradict the assumptions underlying the design of industrial jobs. The more rapidly technology advances, the more frequently jobs are going to be redesigned, and the greater the need for discovering how in fact workers do respond to variations in technologically determined task attributes. In short, we stress the influence of technology in this research, but we want to remember that in any concrete case many environmental, individual, and social characteristics are interacting with economic and technical aspects in influencing over-all response to the job. We believe that technology is important but so are many other things, and the influence of

---

[6] Whyte and others (1955) have well demonstrated this point. See also Whyte (1959) and (1961).

technology on worker response is probably different from what has often been assumed.

Related Research on Job Technology

The relevance of technology to organizational behavior has been demonstrated in a wide variety of research studies over the last 10 or 15 years. Some of this work has examined these factors across a broad range of industries and technologies. For instance, Kerr and Siegel explain the greater "propensity to strike" in industries such as mining, merchant marine, dock working, and lumber, by the worker's relationship to the larger society and also by the "nature of the job [which] determines, by selection and conditioning, the kinds of workers employed and their attitudes." [7] Or, to take another example, consider workers' reaction to differences in supervisory behavior. Studies of response to different styles of supervision ("production-centered" vs. "people-centered," etc.) have produced somewhat contradictory results, partly because of the simultaneous influence of differences in the nature of the task. "Close supervision" is apparently resented more strongly on complex than on simple jobs, assuming an equivalent need or expectation for independence and autonomy on the part of the workers involved.[8] Without due consideration of the influence of job design variables it is difficult to explain some apparent inconsistencies in research findings on questions of this kind.

Many commentators on the nature of modern industrial work, such as those already cited, emphasize the "de-humanizing" effect of the scientific management tradition. Industrial engineers, it is said, have accepted too uncritically the principle first stated by Fayol (1908) and Taylor (1911) that jobs should be designed to be as simple as possible, requiring the lowest feasible amount of skill and initiative. Some of

[7] Kerr and Siegel (1954), p. 195.

[8] Likert (1961) and Zander and Quinn (1962) provide recent summaries of the work on this and related questions by the Survey Research Center of the University of Michigan.

the most outspoken criticism of the adverse human effects of job design based upon the traditional principles of scientific management has recently been coming from within the industrial engineering profession itself.[9] For example, when human response to the characteristics of work is adequately considered, extreme task simplification becomes less economically and technically efficient than had previously been assumed, according to recent studies of job design directed by L. E. Davis of the Industrial Engineering Department of the University of California.[10]

The need for engineers to apply to their work in industry a higher degree of knowledge and skill concerning its human and social impact has also become an important theme of industrial sociology, as illustrated in the work of Merton (1957),[11] Walker (1954), and Roethlisberger.[12] Equally, important, of course, is the need for social scientists working in the industrial context to be conversant with the work and thinking of engineers, as these same authors also emphasize. As Mary Parker Follett stressed, when Industrial Engineering was still young and before Organizational Behavior was conceived as a separate field of study, the facts of technology and the facts of human behavior are still both relevant; the need is to keep them usefully related to each other.[13] Walker has made the same point: "Since the engineering categories with which men built the factory and organized it have developed for the most part without reference to categories based on human behavior — except in a casual and random fashion — and since the categories and abstractions of social science have for the most part developed with only casual contact with

    9 See, for example, the work of Abruzzi (1956) and Gillespie (1948) and (1951).
    10 Davis (1957a, 1957b, 1962); Davis and Canter (1955); Davis, Canter, and Hoffman (1955); Davis and Werling (1960).
    11 "The Machine, the Worker, and the Engineer" (1957), pp. 562–573.
    12 See, for example, Roethlisberger (1941), pp. 36–37, *et passim* on "The relationship between the technologist and the worker."
    13 See Metcalf and Urwick (1940), p. 124.

technological and engineering developments, the necessity arises of bringing them together into a working relationship." [14]

A growing awareness of the relevance of job attributes for human motivation has in recent years stimulated a considerable amount of writing on "job enlargement." [15] These authors have argued, with examples from companies such as IBM and Detroit Edison, that when jobs are made less repetitive, the level of worker motivation and task-involvement improves. Counterclaims have also been made,[16] and in spite of the considerable publicity given to successful examples of enlarging the scope of the task, experiments in this direction have not been widely imitated; apparently the evidence has not been entirely convincing, perhaps because the problem is somewhat more complex than it first appeared.

As a further example of recent interest in the general field of human response to technology at the work level, we should mention the large literature on the subject of the effects of automation. Most of this writing concerns how automation will influence levels of employment rather than the effect of automation on workers' response to the characteristics of automated jobs; much of this writing is based more on speculation than on concrete research. The general trend emerging from a relatively small number of concrete case studies on the subject is not clear, although usually less interaction and a decreased feeling of autonomy and of direct contact with the process have been mentioned; predictions that shifting to automation would involve a significant increase in skill requirements have usually *not* been supported by these studies.[17]

14 Walker (1951), p. 211.

15 This literature is quite extensive; recommended references include Bibby (1955); Elliott (1953); Fogarty (1956), pp. 140–147; and Walker (1950a).

16 Kennedy and O'Neill (1958); Kilbridge (1961a), (1961b).

17 Bright (1958a) Chapter 12, "The Impact of Automation on the Work Force," pp. 170–197; Bright (1958b); Buckingham (1961) Chapter 5, "Auto-

Two research groups have been especially important in the development of the thinking which underlies our present research: The Tavistock Institute in London and the Technology Project of the Institute of Human Relations at Yale.

The Tavistock group have repeatedly emphasized the interaction among technological, social, and psychological determinants of organizational behavior, and have applied this "socio-technical system" concept in impressive action-research projects in a wide range of technological settings, most notably in British coal mining [18] and Indian Textile manufacture.[19] We have been influenced by their stress on technology's interaction with personal and social determinants of behavior and by their attention to the importance of understanding the inherent characteristics of the "whole task" when analyzing industrial jobs.

The work of Charles Walker and his colleagues at Yale, in which one of us participated, has consistently emphasized the importance of understanding the impact of "the immediate job," that is, the intrinsic attributes of the task to be performed. The published studies of this group have been primarily concerned with automobile assembly [20] and steel manufacture,[21] but their work has in fact been applied to a number of widely differing technologies as well, including office equipment, [22] chemicals, aircraft engines, banking, and, more recently, electronics assembly.[23] Not only the emphasis

---

mation and the Worker," pp. 93–108; Faunce (1958a) (1958b); Mann and Hoffman (1960); Mann and Williams (1962); Naville (1960); Shultz and Weber (1960); Society for Applied Anthropology (1956); U.S. Bureau of Labor Statistics (1955–1958).

[18] Trist and Bamforth (1951); Trist and others (1963); see also Hill and Trist (1962).

[19] Rice (1958); see also Rice (1963).

[20] Guest (1955a, 1955b); Jasinski (1956); Turner (1955a, 1957); Walker and Guest (1952); Walker, Guest, and Turner (1956); Whyte (1961), pp. 179–197.

[21] Walker (1950b), (1957).

[22] Richardson and Walker (1948); Walker (1950a).

[23] Turner and Miclette (1962).

of this group but also some of their specific procedures for studying technological determinants of behavior are reflected in our present research, as will be indicated below.

Research Design and Methodology

As already explained, our purpose was to develop and implement a method of measuring job attributes that would help predict workers' response to their jobs across a wide range of differing technologies. The research study involved the following phases:

1. To develop a preliminary conceptual scheme with which to investigate the interrelationships among the various dependent, independent, and supplementary variables in which we were interested. More will be said about this step below.
2. To conceptualize and select the key task attributes to be studied and to develop scales for their measurement; to develop a questionnaire to be administered to workers to measure some of their responses and certain supplementary variables.
3. To test and improve, by means of a pilot study [24] in two companies in the same industry, the utility of our task attribute scales and questionnaire.
4. To select for study a sample of about 50 jobs in order to provide a wide range in type of company, location, technology, and task attributes. (Eventually usable data on 470 men on 47 jobs in 11 companies were collected. Because we found it difficult, in the pilot study, to isolate the effect of sex difference on the other variables we were studying, we decided to confine the major survey to jobs on which only men were employed.)
5. To collect the primary data of the study by scoring the attributes of the 47 jobs, examining company records, and administering the questionnaires to the 470 men in our final sample. (We found that it was not possible to

[24] The results of this pilot study are not incorporated in the present report. They have been reported in a doctoral dissertation by Laurent Picard (1964).

secure reliable and comparable data from company records on either turnover or worker productivity.)

6. To analyze the resulting data and plan their presentation. This step is explained in more detail below.

Scheme for Relating Key Variables

The planning for this research started with the concept
that every industrial job contained certain technologically determined intrinsic task attributes which would influence
workers' response. By "intrinsic task attributes" we meant
such characteristics of the job as the amount of variety, autonomy, responsibility, and interaction with others built into
its design. We conceived of these task attributes as by no
means the only relevant determinants of response to work,
but as worth more systematic attention across a wide range
of technological settings than it seemed to us they had yet
received in existing research. We recognized that in actual-
ity how a given worker "responded" to his job, for example,
how much satisfaction he expressed with it and whether or
not he was frequently absent from work, would depend not
only upon the intrinsic attributes of his immediate task at
work, but also upon many other influences on his behavior,
such as management's policy and practice, supervisory behavior, economic and social conditions in the larger environment, pay, and his individual background, needs, predispositions, etc. Furthermore, we recognized that even if it were
possible to take into account all these determinants of behavior and how they interacted with one another, any prediction from them to the worker's ultimate behavior (response) would be a risky leap, since how all these and other
influences actually operated would depend in fact upon the
social organization(s) to which he belonged and the developing pattern of interpersonal relationships, norms, and values
at work.

In other words, our over-all procedure was as indicated in
Exhibit 1.1. We were to study the relationship between task

Exhibit 1.1

OVER-ALL STRATEGY

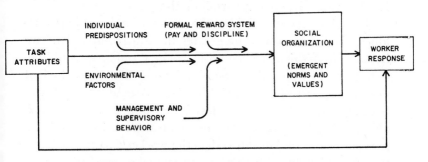

attributes and worker response, while recognizing that in fact worker response would be largely determined by the total pattern of social organization at work, and that this in turn would be influenced not only by task attributes but also by a number of other important classes of variables, individual, environmental, and organizational. We realized that others had tried unsuccessfully to make this leap from "determinants" of behavior to final response, without studying how the determinants were mediated through social organization at work. Nevertheless, we believed the attempt worthwhile because, as explained below, the particular manner in which we planned to study task attributes had not been attempted before, and because we hoped to design our study so as to control most of the other influences on worker response. Even the failure of such an attempt would, we felt, make a useful contribution. Before discussing the extent to which it did succeed or fail, we need to present more detail about the different variables we attempted to measure and how we conceived their interrelationship.

For the purpose of this study we chose to conceive all the attributes of the task that we measured as independent variables. Later in this chapter we will describe how we conceptualized and measured these task attributes, and how we combined them into an index that we came to call the Requisite Task Attribute Index (RTA Index). We hypothesized that this set of independent variables would be positively related to three dependent variables, the greater the magnitude of the independent variables, the greater the dependent variables. In other words, the greater the job "complexity," we hypothesized, the more favorable workers' response would be, as measured by these dependent variables. The two principal dependent or response variables were Attendance and Job Satisfaction; and the third, less important, dependent variable was Psychosomatic Response, a measure of freedom from nervousness or nervous disorders the worker experienced and traced to his job. (In this report we make very little use of this measure, mostly because preliminary analysis raised difficult questions as to its validity.) Our Job Satisfaction measure was an index composed of five questions from the questionnaire. (See Appendix A for the specific questions used in this and other questionnaire indices.) As an Attendance measure we used the company's records of the number of times (not days) the man had been absent during the prior twelve months. The use of the "times absent" measure tended to eliminate any exaggerated effect from a single long illness.[25]

We also conceived of four sets of "supplementary variables" that could importantly influence the relationship between our independent and dependent variables. The first set of such supplementary variables was a group of situational factors that, according to other research, influence attendance and job satisfaction: the immediate supervisor, the immediate work group, the company, the union, and the level of pay. Instead of trying to measure these variables directly, we obtained data on the first four by using questions in the written questionnaire that elicited the workers' feeling of satisfaction with these factors. This gave us measures of Company Satisfaction (five questions), Foreman Satisfaction (four ques-

[25] This method of utilizing absenteeism records was well justified in the wartime studies directed by Mayo. See Fox and Scott (1943).

tions) , Work Group Satisfaction (four questions) , and Union Satisfaction (one question) . Pay could, of course, be measured directly.

The second set of supplementary variables consisted of four measures of the characteristics of the individual worker: his age, his highest level of formal education, his years of seniority with the company, and his score on a series of questions in the questionnaire selected to give some clue to his personality tendencies. The worker's age and seniority were obtained from company records, as well as from the man himself. The personality test selected was 24 items from the positive F-scale, the so-called measure of authoritarian personality.[26]

The third set of supplementary variables was of a special kind that we called the Perceived Task Attributes. We hypothesized that workers would be influenced by the attributes of their task but that this influence would, in effect, be filtered through their perception of the task, *their* mental image of work that would inevitably be different to some degree from the picture of the work captured by the researchers' systematic but relatively simple measurement methods. We wanted to measure how the workers perceived the attributes of their own job so we could clarify whether deviance from our hypothesized causal relation was due to perceptual differences or truly different responses. For this purpose we used one set of questionnaire answers (eight questions) to construct a Perceived Task Index (PT Index) that emphasized the activities required by the job. We used a different set of questionnaire responses to construct a Perceived Opportunity to Contribute Index (POC Index) (three questions) that emphasized the degree to which the job was perceived as providing a chance for the worker to utilize his ideas and skills.

Exhibit 1.2 presents in schematic form these sets of variables and the way the researchers conceived of their interrelationship. As each of these variables is brought up for dis-

[26] Adorno and others (1950) ; Christie and Jahoda (1954) .

Exhibit 1.2

KEY VARIABLES AND THEIR INTERRELATIONSHIPS

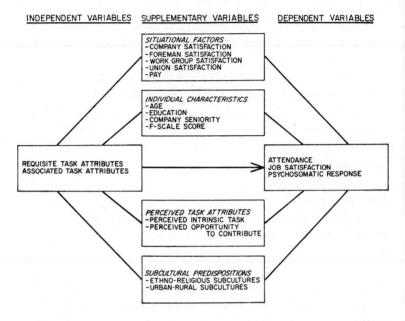

cussion in later chapters, the way they were measured will be explained in more detail.

As indicated in Exhibit 1.2, before we completed the study we found we needed to add to our original scheme a fourth type of supplementary variable to help account for our findings. This variable of Subcultural Predispositions was needed to trace the supplementary influence of subcultures, defined either by ethno-religious differences or by the urban or rural nature of the work setting.

A word of explanation concerning the supplementary influence of these subcultural differences will be helpful at this point. To preview very briefly ground that will be covered in detail in later chapters, we discovered no significant relationship in our total population between task attributes and worker response measured in terms of job satisfaction. Remembering the "risky leap" referred to above, we then hypothesized that two different predispositions to work might have developed from the values and norms emerging within the social organizations of the different plants which constituted our research sites. So we separated the research sites into two groups based on ethno-religious and rural-urban subcultures. We then discovered that the original hypothesis concerning the relationship between job complexity and satisfaction was confirmed within the rural subcultures, whereas when the subculture was predominantly urban, satisfaction was higher on simple than on complex jobs. We will have much more to say about this finding later on, how we obtained it and what it seems to mean. The purpose of mentioning it here is simply to explain that Subcultural Predispositions were *not* in our original design and were introduced essentially in order to deal with a negative finding in the total sample on the relationship between task attributes and job satisfaction. Also perhaps this little preview will make it easier for the reader to see "where we're going" as he covers some of the more detailed material that has to be dealt with before we properly get there.

Analysis of the Data

The task attribute scores, questionnaire responses, and attendance data were punched on IBM cards, and means, deviations, and intercorrelation matrices were run on all variables. Among other things this showed clearly that there was a strong co-variance among the various task attributes that we had scored; jobs scoring high on one attribute tended to have high scores on all the other attributes as well. This made it difficult to give as much attention as we had hoped to the differential effects of our various task attributes, but it did mean that for much of our subsequent analysis we could combine our attribute scores into an over-all Requisite Task Attribute Index, which constituted a general measure of over-all job complexity. Preliminary analysis also showed that the Rated

Task Attribute scores were closely related to the Perceived Task Attribute scores. This indicated that our rating procedure was illuminating differences between jobs which workers themselves perceived and considered relevant. Furthermore, the response measures we obtained from the various questionnaire items were related to each other in a way which suggested that the questionnaire itself was a reasonably reliable indication of workers' attitudes, although we soon discovered that the questionnaire measured a different kind of response than did the attendance data. (This finding is discussed in detail in later chapters.)

The distribution of most of our variables was far from "normal," and it appeared that the intercorrelations given us by the computer would not be an appropriate medium for presenting our findings. In analyzing relationships between different job attributes, it was relatively simple to compute rank correlations for the 47 jobs. Almost all of the other data to be presented in this report will be based on contingency tables, with Chi Square values being used to test the strength of association between two variables.

Ways of Conceptualizing the Nature of Industrial Work

In order to learn more about the relationship between the nature of work and the response of workers, it was first necessary to conceptualize and measure those attributes or requirements of industrial work that were most likely to influence worker response. We now need to report in more detail how this research step was taken.

In order to take this step it was necessary to establish criteria for selecting the descriptive framework. For one thing, the descriptive scheme should be able to characterize in the same terms jobs from across the entire range of industrial experience. It should describe jobs in terms that were quantifiable at least to a first approximation. It should be able to describe jobs in behavioral terms: what concrete human behavior needs to be carried out if the work is to be performed.

For this purpose behavior should be defined broadly so as not only to include the necessary motor activities but also the necessary social and mental behaviors. Finally, the descriptive scheme should be practical to use on the factory floor with a modest investment of scoring time, and with reliability as between different scorers.

Of course, the researchers were aware of the prior existence of a number of ways of describing work that for years have been widely used in industry for some very practical purposes. To what extent did these methods meet our criteria?

Work has traditionally been described in industry from a number of standpoints of which the four most widely used can be characterized as technical, organizational, social, and personal. Most business organizations use different documents to define work in these traditional ways. Manufacturing shops use operation sheets to describe jobs from a *technical* standpoint. These sheets list the sequence of operations to be performed, but a typical entry, such as "Rough turn the 10-inch flange," says more about what end result the worker is expected to get the machine to produce than what behavior the worker himself needs to engage in. Formal statements of job descriptions are used to define work from an *organizational* standpoint. They usually define jobs in terms of larger organizational purposes, and they tell how each job has a function and a relation to other jobs in the achievement of this purpose. Jobs are defined *socially*, not only by the informal status rankings they are assigned by general opinion, but more formally by job evaluation schemes. As the name implies, these schemes are used to evaluate jobs for payment purposes by ranking them in terms of qualities that are generally considered by society to be desirable. Jobs are also defined in *personal* terms, in terms of a person's expected career progression through time. For instance, a draftsman, in describing his job, would place himself in the progression of drafting apprentice, detailer, No. 2 designer, and No. 1 designer. These job sequences are sometimes formalized on paper as promotion ladders. All these traditional ways of describing industrial work have some behavioral description in them, but none of them really concentrates on describing the human behavior that needs to be engaged in if the task is to be performed. They are also limited, for our purposes, by their resistance to comparative measurement.

One special variant of describing work from a technical standpoint has been the micro-motion study of work [27] and the way this has been extended into human engineering or human factors study.[28] This approach conceives of the worker as a physiological or neuro-mechanical apparatus with certain limits as to what he can and cannot do under given conditions. In turn, it describes work in terms of its relationship to these physiological limits. "In a human engineering context, human beings are considered as being part of a man-machine system." [29] This approach describes work in behavioral terms, but only in regard to human limits with little attention to the effects of intermediate levels of required motor behavior. It does not usually describe jobs in regard to necessary social behavior or to the necessary use of higher mental processes, or to the inevitable effects on motivation of attitudes derived from the nature of the task.

At the other extreme from micro-motion approaches to job description are some recent systematic studies on organizational behavior that are focused primarily on other organizational variables such as leadership styles or organizational structure and their relation to output variables such as productivity and satisfaction. These studies, while not focusing on the nature of work, have often been forced to categorize

[27] See the critiques of "micromotionism" by Albruzzi (1956) and Gillespie (1951). Micro-motion analysis has grown out of efforts to assign standard times to job performance through analyzing the motions required to perform the work. For a standard text on this subject, see Maynard, Stegmerten, and Schwab (1948).

[28] Bennett (1963); Fleishman (1961), Section nine, "Engineering Psychology," pp. 579–633; McCormick (1957).

[29] Tiffin and McCormick (1958), p. 460.

and roughly compare the kinds of work being done in the organizational settings under study. For this purpose they resort to such global descriptive terms as repetitive, monotonous, creative, simple, intricate, routine, etc. The chief criticism of such categories for systematic description is, of course, that they are not precise enough to reduce to specific measurement operations.

This brief review of existing schemes for describing work indicates the general issue the researchers faced in devising a new, useful way of measuring and talking about industrial work. We approached this aspect of our work with a search of the literature for useful ideas, a reflective review of our own experiences as students of industrial work, and by the trial and error process of attempting to define and actually measure a wide variety of task attributes. This process of refinement went on primarily during the pilot study stage, but continued to some extent throughout the study. The resulting scheme in its present form should therefore be looked at as an interim stage in the continuing process of clarifying and refining these variables.

A Behavioral Conceptualization of Work

In searching for an approach to describing work in behavioral terms, the researchers found it useful to use the categorization of the elements of human behavior developed by Homans (1950). Exhibit 1.3 presents a diagram of the descriptive scheme that was finally selected, and it can be seen that the three rows are headed by the three elements of behavior used by Homans. Activities refers to what people do in the sense of walking, manipulating tools, etc. Interactions refers to any contact between people, whether by word or gesture, in which there is an overt acknowledgment of a human exchange. Mental States (originally called sentiments by Homans) refers to any mental state or process suggested by such terms as attitude, feeling, awareness, cognition, etc.

The diagram also indicates that we conceptualized two

Exhibit 1.3

REQUISITE TASK ATTRIBUTES: DESCRIPTIVE SCHEME

ELEMENTS OF BEHAVIOR

		ACTIVITIES	INTERACTIONS	MENTAL STATES
ELEMENTS OF TASK	PRESCRIBED	VARIETY (OBJECT AND MOTOR)	REQUIRED INTERACTION	KNOWLEDGE AND SKILL
	DISCRETIONARY	AUTONOMY	OPTIONAL INTERACTION (ON OR OFF THE JOB)	RESPONSIBILITY

fundamentally different aspects of every human task, Prescribed and Discretionary. By Prescribed we mean that part of the task behavior that is programmed, predesigned, or predetermined. By Discretionary behavior we mean that within the prescribed limits certain other behavior can exist at the discretion of the individual. What is prescribed sets boundaries within which what is discretionary can occur. This distinction was developed by Wilfred Brown, who defined these two major components of work as follows: "The prescribed components — those things that the person in the role must do; and the discretionary component of work — those decisions or choices that the person in the role must take." [30]

[30] Brown (1960), p. 21. Note that Brown's "discretionary" behavior is still "required" in Homans' sense. Our scheme was not designed to take account of what Homans called "emergent behavior," although in the case of Interaction we were forced to consider the emergent aspects, as explained below.

Once these two ways of categorizing behavior and tasks were selected, it was possible to ask, what are the prescribed activities, interactions, and mental states and in turn the discretionary aspects? In each of the cells in the diagram is indicated the term the researchers came to apply to each of these six attributes of industrial work.

In choosing the term Variety for the first of these cells the researchers were using it in its everyday meaning and were thinking of the entire range of different activities that can be prescribed by various job designs.[31] This ranges, for instance, from the often cited assembly line worker attaching a nut to a bolt time after time to such high variety industrial jobs as those of model shop machinists. The researchers chose to measure this major attribute by combining the scores of two individual attributes, Motor Variety and Object Variety.

The term Autonomy refers to the discretion the worker is expected to exercise (assumed in the design of the job) in carrying out the assigned task activities. This would include the degree of choice or judgment necessary in regard to the quality of material used, selection of appropriate tools, and

[31] Since the early work of Mayo and the British Industrial Fatigue Research Board, the effect on worker response of different degrees of variety in work has been a major focus of research in this field. In interviews with 976 men in two automobile and one metal fabrication plant, Wyatt and Marriott (1956) replicated the finding of Walker and Guest (1952) that interest and monotony were principal sources of satisfaction and dissatisfaction. All these sources, as well as other studies, stress two important aspects of response to variety: (1) when the general level of variety is low, a small difference between jobs makes a large difference to workers' response; (2) for a significant number of workers lack of variety is *not* a source of dissatisfaction. (This "adjusted" response to low variety will be discussed in a later chapter.) See also Turner and Miclette (1962). In connection with these points, Chinoy (1952) and (1955) and Guest (1954) have each stressed the comparatively "limited" aspirations of automobile workers, especially those with long seniority. It should also be noted that some recent studies have failed to show a clear relationship between repetitiveness and worker response, apparently because other factors were more important in the particular situations that were studied, e.g. Kilbridge (1961a) and (1961b); Kennedy and O'Neill (1958).

the sequence in which different parts of the task were performed. Here we were thinking of a range from work with low autonomy even if highly varied, such as the highly programmed job of a missile crewman performing a count-down, to work requiring considerable exercise of judgment as to quality, methods, etc., such as a high-quality glass blower's job.[32]

In regard to Required Interaction, the researchers were concerned with the amount of necessary interdependence between tasks, particularly that kind of interdependence for which direct face-to-face communication is needed to perform the task properly.[33] The communication (or interaction) could be required either to solve a job problem or to exchange task relevant information; in other words, the kind necessary between an open hearth operator and his helper about how to handle a furnace blister or the kind required between two long-distance telephone operators.

In developing ideas about Optional Interaction the researchers found it impossible to maintain the purity of their distinction between behavior requisite to task performance and other behavior during work. The technical structure of any task sets up some constraints or limits to the amount of interaction that workers can engage in at will. For instance, the machinery can be in a position to prevent interaction, or it can create noise which hinders it. Earlier studies had impressed us with the importance that such variations in constraints to nonprescribed interaction could have on actual be-

[32] Whyte (1957) found that high-quality glass blowers, in discussing the various jobs to which they were assigned, valued such attributes as creativity, achievement, contribution, as well as variety and lack of "problems." Blauner (1960) is one of many writers on the subject who have stressed the extent to which a favorable response to work is related to the degree of control which the worker perceives he exercises over his own activities on the job.

[33] The importance of the pattern of interaction required by the task as a determinant of job attitude has been emphasized by Whyte (1948, 1961) and Miller (1958–1959) among others.

havior.[34] In other words, certain requisites of the task (such as machinery layout or noise) could limit interaction behavior which, while not directly essential to task accomplishment, might nevertheless influence task performance and response in important ways. So we included the idea of Optional Interaction in our task attribute scheme in order to study the impact of these technologically determined interaction restraints. For this purpose we measured Optional Interaction both on the job and off the job.

The researchers found that there were a number of ways to approach specifying those prescribed mental states that are necessary for task performance. We wanted to capture, in this cell of our task attribute scheme, the kind of mental preparation or readiness that could be quite specifically prescribed in advance as essential in order to perform the job adequately.[35] This would include (for a carburetor assembler, for example) not only specific items of knowledge (what parts are needed and in what positions), but also the motor skills needed to actually fit the pieces together. Instead of trying to measure directly all the complex aspects of these knowledge and skill requirements we chose, as an indirect index of them, to measure the length of time it was expected

[34] The early British studies of reactions to repetitive work (Great Britain Industrial Health (Fatigue) Research Board, Reports No. 26, 30, 56, 77, for example) had frequently stressed the importance of social interaction as an antidote to monotony. Many more recent studies have made the same point, and have noted how certain technologies erect barriers to the kind of interaction that counteracts negative response to repetitiveness. See, for example, Cox (1953) ; Cox and Dyce Sharp (1951) ; Jasinski (1956) ; Roy (1959–1960) ; Sayles (1954) and (1958), p. 93; Ulrich, Booz, and Lawrence (1950) ; Wyatt and Marriott (1956), pp. 31, 39–40; Zaleznik (1956), espec. pp. 118–125.

[35] Many previous studies had emphasized the importance of level of required skill in influencing response to work. For example, Kasl and French (1962) found that "skill level is inversely related to dispensary visits" (p. 79) ; and Fraser, in a sample of 3,000 British workers during World War II, found that a skill level inappropriate to the individual's intelligence was one of several factors significantly related to the incidence of neurosis. (Great Britain Industrial Health (Fatigue) Research Board, Report No. 90, 1947.)

to take a person to learn how to perform all aspects of the task proficiently.

The sixth cell in our scheme involves discretionary mental states. For us this connoted attitudes or feeling states that were necessary for task performance but that did not lend themselves to preprogramming — that is, they remained in a sense optional even though "necessary." Responsibility was the label that seemed most appropriate to the researchers to characterize the discretionary mental states we were interested in measuring. No matter how much the designer of a job wishes to "require" a certain kind of responsible attitude for the job to be performed, the feeling of responsibility actually present remains "discretionary" in the sense that it cannot be prescribed or programmed as can variety or required interaction, for example, or even learning time. Yet an analysis of the job can yield an estimate of the sense of responsibility called for by the job design, or potentially applicable in effectively performing the work. It seemed to the researchers that the more ambiguity associated with what to do when something goes wrong, the greater the probability of serious damage or personal injury, and the longer the time after completing a job before small mistakes can be detected, the greater is (can be) the sense of responsibility associated with the work. The Responsibility Index we constructed is therefore made up of three individual job attributes: Probability of Serious Error, Ambiguity of Remedial Action, and Time Span of Discretion.[36]

In addition to these six attributes that are required by the intrinsic nature of the task, the researchers developed five additional measures of attributes that were intimately associated with the nature of the job but were not requisite to its performance, which we called the Associated Task Attributes. The principal one of these attributes was the Task Identity Index. This index pulls together four independent

---

[36] For the concept Time Span of Discretion and for the way of measuring it, we drew directly on the work of Elliot Jaques (1956 and 1961).

measures of how clearly any given task can be differentiated as a unique and visible work assignment.[37] The other associated job attributes that were measured were Pay, Working Conditions, Cycle Time,[38] Level of Mechanization, and Capital Investment. It can readily be seen how each of these job associated attributes can take on symbolic meanings that are important to the worker and his response to the job.

Exhibits 1.4 and 1.5 summarize briefly how all the task attributes, both requisite and associated, were defined and how some of them were developed as indices of several underlying indicators. Appendix B describes in more detail the methods used for measuring these attributes and refers to some other attributes the researchers experimented with and eliminated. It need only be stated here that the measurement scales for all the attributes except Pay, Level of Mechanization, and Capital Investment were consistently designed to range in points from 1 to 9, with 1 representing the least conceivable amount of the attribute concerned and 9 representing the most conceivable amount. In certain instances the scales used a geometric rather than an arithmetic progression.

[37] This index was based on the idea that seeing the results of one's work and experiencing a sense of closure in regard to it were important to most people. Interviews with automobile assembly workers had shown that visibility of a worker's operation in the completed product could be a source of satisfaction on otherwise disliked tasks. The same notion is relevant to the concept of "traction" developed by Baldamus (1951 and 1961) especially in the "pull towards completing" an object or batch of objects that can be experienced positively on repetitive work. The relevance of a sense of completeness or closure is stressed by Gillespie (1951), and in the Tavistock studies on the extent to which the worker "can experience . . . the completion of a 'whole' task." (Rice, 1958, p. 36.)

[38] For a time we believed that Cycle Time might be a useful measure of repetitiveness or variety. However, we often found it very difficult to decide which of several different "cycles" on a particular job was in fact most relevant psychologically. In spite of this difficulty, other studies have shown that even small differences in cycle are significantly associated with worker response, especially when the tasks are similar in other respects. See, for example, Wyatt and Marriott (1956), pp. 22–23, and Cox and Dyce Sharp (1951).

Exhibit 1.4

LIST OF REQUISITE TASK ATTRIBUTES

ACTIVITY
  Object Variety
  The number of parts, tools, and controls to be manipulated.
  Motor Variety — average of:
    Variety in Prescribed Work Pace
    Variety in Physical Location of Work
    Variety of Prescribed Physical Operations of Work
  Autonomy — average of:
    Amount of worker latitude in selection of work methods
    Amount of worker latitude in selection of work sequence
    Amount of worker latitude in selection of work pace
    Amount of worker latitude in accepting or rejecting the quality of
      incoming materials
    Amount of worker choice in securing outside services

INTERACTION
  Required Interaction — average of:
    Number of people required to interact with, at least every two
      hours
    Quantity of time spent in required interactions
  Optional Interaction On-the-Job — average of:
    Number of people available for interaction in working area
    Quantity of time available for interaction while working
  Optional Interaction Off-the-Job
    Amount of time worker is free to choose to leave the work area
      without reprimand

MENTAL STATES
  Knowledge and Skill
    Amount of time required to learn to perform job proficiently
  Responsibility — average of:
    Ambiguity of Remedial Action (to correct routine job problems)
    Time Span of Discretion — (maximum time before marginal sub-
      standard work is detected)
    Probability of Serious (harmful or costly) Error

In developing their thinking about these job attributes and
their underlying indicators, the researchers drew on a number of prior studies of technology. In particular, the index
of "mass production factors" used by Walker and Guest
(1952) contained many items that have been carried over in
modified form into the task attribute list. Their factor of

Exhibit 1.5

LIST OF ASSOCIATED TASK ATTRIBUTES

Task Identity — average of:
   Clarity of Cycle Closure
   Visibility of Transformation (performed by the worker)
   Visibility (of work transformation) in the Finished Product
   Magnitude of (value added by the) Transformation
Pay
   Average weekly gross pay without overtime adjusted for U.S. and
      Canadian differential
Working Conditions — average of:
   Amount of light and cleanliness in general work area
   Amount of fumes, etc.
   Temperature
   Amount of dirt, grease, oil, in immediate job area
Cycle Time
   Length in time of major work cycle
Level of Mechanization
   Jobs ranked by the technical sophistication of the machinery em-
      ployed *
Capital Investment
   Jobs ranked by estimated amount of capital invested per worker

   * Bright's scale of 17 "levels of mechanization" was used as a guide in ranking our 47 jobs. See Bright (1958), pp. 41–46.

"repetitiveness" is related to our Variety attribute; their "mechanical pacing" is related to our Autonomy attribute; their "skill" is the same as our Knowledge and Skill; and their factors of "frequency of social interaction" and "size of inter-acting group" are related to our Interaction measures. Since they were studying only automobile assembly jobs, their measurement techniques were less applicable to the wide range of jobs in the present study. The concept of Time Span of Discretion has been taken directly from the work of Elliot Jaques. The concept that Baldamus developed of "traction," the "feeling of being pulled along by the inertia inherent in a particular activity" [39] is related to our attributes of Variety and Clarity of Cycle Closure.

   The six attributes requisite to task performance that were

[39] Baldamus (1961), p. 59. See also Baldamus (1951).

selected for systematic study do not, of course, capture even in a simplified form all the ways tasks establish requirements for the behavior of workers. A brief review of some of these other possibilities and the reasons for their exclusion can provide added perspective on what was selected for study. The study could have given attention to the amount of physical or muscular effort required by the task. A study of the required hours of work per day or week could have been done. The study could have examined the requirement the task placed upon the different sense organs of the worker. This approach, for instance, could have examined the eye focusing requirements in terms of distance, movement, and time. Attention could have been given to dexterity requirements or tactile sensitivity. The fact that some jobs more than others require workers to expose themselves to possible bodily harm could have been studied. Jobs vary in the way they require workers to adapt to unpredictable work interruptions and to tolerate high rates of quality rejections due to variables beyond their control. Some interest could have been taken in the aesthetic appeal of different kinds of work, such as the appeal of glass blowing versus coal mining. More attention could have been given to the characteristics of the work related interactions — were they with people holding jobs with different or similar technical requirements and social status. All of these alternatives were eliminated primarily for the same basic reason: the researchers did not think these attributes would have any discernible influence on worker response, given the range of variance that could be expected in a sample of modern industrial jobs. A secondary reason was that some of these alternative attributes presented particularly difficult measurement problems. None of our subsequent observations has caused us to question the original judgment to exclude these possible attributes.

Characteristics of the Jobs Studied

The 47 jobs in our sample were drawn from 11 companies, deliberately selected to secure broad diversification as to technology and nature of the work, as well as to company size, community size, and regional setting. This means that the sample selected offers a reasonable picture of the range of industrial work, but it does not necessarily represent the distribution of job characteristics across North American industry.

One way the reader can judge for himself the range or coverage of jobs studied is to consider the list of industries studied (see Exhibit 1.6) against his own knowledge of the

Exhibit 1.6

INDUSTRIES AND NUMBER OF JOBS IN SAMPLE

Industry	Number of Jobs
Aluminum Rolling and Extruding	6
Baking	4
Bottling	2
Large Household Appliance	5
Hardware	4
Paper (Book Grades)	5
Paper (Newsprint Grades)	3
Plastic and Fiber Utensils	5
Railroad	7
Tin Plate Containers	4
Textile Weaving	2
Total	47

diversity of North American industry. Another way to judge the range is to analyze this list against the numerous ways industries are typified in common usage. Industries are known as soft or hard goods industries, and in this regard we can point to textiles on the one hand and hardware on the other. Another breakdown is the threefold one: mass production, job shop, and continuous process.[40] The tin plate container producer would represent mass production in our sample and

40 See, for example, Woodward (1958).

the book grade paper firm works mostly to unique customer specifications in a job shop fashion. The best example of continuous process type in our sample is newsprint grade paper and aluminum fabricating. The railroads represent a service industry as against the rest, which produce more tangible products. Sometimes distinctions are made between science-based industries and industries oriented to traditional methods. In our sample this split is represented by the heavy use of science and engineering in aluminum and paper as against the more traditional ways of railroads and textiles. Industries with a very short product-in-process time, such as the bakery (less than a day) are represented, as against the long product-in-process represented by large appliances. Of course, many industries of such obvious importance as steel, automotive, oil, and chemical are not represented, but at least some of their distinctive kinds of jobs and technology are represented.

Data on the range and distribution within the 47 job samples of the various requisite and associated task attributes are given in Appendix C. In general, as shown in Appendix C, the distribution across the 47 jobs of our measures for most task attributes was relatively "flat." In other words, our sample included enough jobs with high, medium, and low scores on the various attributes to provide a reasonable sample of a relatively broad range of task attributes. However, there were very few jobs at the extreme "high" end of the scales we used for certain task attributes, especially Autonomy, Required Interaction, and Responsibility. This means that we found less of these particular attributes in our sample than we expected, since the attribute scales were originally designed to cover the range of from the "least" to the "most" of each attribute that could normally be expected in a broad sample of industrial "blue collar" work. On the other hand, the distribution of Associated Task Attributes, Clarity of Cycle Closure and Visibility of Transformation, "peaked" to the right, indicating that low Task Identity was not a problem for most of the jobs in our sample. (See Appendix C for detail on these distributions, and Appendix B for an explanation of the meaning of the various parts on each of the attribute scales.)

The Requisite Task Attribute Index

The various measures of task attributes were closely related to each other, in the sense that a job with a high (or low) score on any one attribute tended to leave high (or low) scores on most of the other attributes as well.

Appendix D presents rank correlations between each of the job attributes that are requisite to task performance. It will immediately be seen that all of these attributes have a strong correlation with one another. The researchers had hypothesized a significant relation among these attributes, but we were surprised by its strength. The strength of these relations ranged from Motor Variety, which had a mean correlation of .57 with all the other attributes, through Object Variety (.50), Optional Interaction On-the-Job (.49), Autonomy (.48), Knowledge and Skill (.48), Required Interaction (.47), and Optional Interaction Off-the-Job (.43).

It can be argued that the strength of these correlations is based on logical causal connections between attributes, such as that between the number of tools, parts, and controls to be used, and the learning time required. Is it logically obvious in the same way, however, that interactions of all kinds would increase with increases in autonomy? It should also be remembered that examples can easily be found of jobs that have all combinations from high to low of these different attributes. The size of the correlations remains as a fact worthy of note, and it suggested to the researchers the eminent practicality of developing a composite index of these attributes.

The RTA Index represents a weighted total of all six of the requisite task attributes. A double weight was assigned to Autonomy and Variety (one weight each for Object and Motor Variety), while all other attributes were given a single weight. The extra weighting to Autonomy and Variety was given partly because these attributes had the strongest correlations with other attributes, but more importantly because of the researchers' judgment that these activity attributes were especially important determinants of worker responses to industrial work. The Optional Interaction attribute was handled by including in the index for each job the larger score as between Optional Interaction On-the-Job and Off-the-Job, since we saw these as alternative ways of exercising interaction discretion. As would, of course, be predicted, the resulting RTA Index had a high correlation with all of its underlying job attributes. (See Appendix D for these data.) The relationship between the RTA Index and the various Associated Task Attributes is worth noting briefly. (Again, the relevant rank correlations are presented in Appendix D.) Surprisingly, there was no significant positive relationship between RTA Index scores and Pay or Working Conditions. (In both cases there was a slight *negative* relationship $(p < .10)$; higher pay and cleaner and more comfortable working conditions were, if anything, associated with *lower* RTA scores.)

Once the RTA Index was computed for each of the 47 jobs, it was possible to rank order the jobs on this single index and begin to use it as a single independent variable to be related to the various dependent and intervening variables. Exhibit 1.7 presents a rank listing of the jobs to provide the reader with a feel for the distribution of the RTA Index and some additional information about the specific jobs studied. It should be remembered in examining the rank list that it would be erroneous to conclude, for instance, that all tool and die jobs would score 59.4 and always outrank loom repairmen. This rank list simply indicates that a particular job, such as a tool and die maker job, in a particular company scored as indicated and outranked other particular jobs as indicated.

Exhibit 1.7

JOBS IN SAMPLE RANKED BY REQUISITE TASK ATTRIBUTE INDEX

Job Title	RTA Index Score
Paper Machine Operator	63
Tool and Die Maker	59.4
Loom Repairman	54
Automatic Screw Machine Operator (including setup)	53
Paper Super Calender Operator (Fine Grades)	52.8
Railroad Sectionman (Maintain Track)	50
Paper Machine Backtender	49
Paper Digester Operator	47.5
Railroad Locomotive Airbrake Repairman	46
Aluminum Extrusion Inspector	44
Aluminum Foil Roller	44
Automatic Screw Machine Operator	42.5
Railroad Blacksmith	42
Generator Armature Winder	41
Aluminum Remelt Furnace Tender	40.9
Aluminum Extrusion Press Operator	39
Telephone Wireman and Pole Climber	37.9
Aluminum Flat Mill Operator	36
Hand Pastry and Roll Maker	35.4
Paper Trimming Machine Operator	35
Textile Tenting Machine Operator	33.2
Bakery Order Filler and Shipper	32
Paper Super Calender Operator (Coarse Grades)	31
Washing Machine Pump Assembler	30
Multiple Utensil Fabricator	29.1
Railroad Track Rebuilding Crewman	29
Railroad Car Airbrake Repairman	27.7
Cake Oven Operator	26
Extrusion Cut-off Saw Operator	26
General Warehouseman and Fork Lift Truck Operator	25.9
Can Packer	25.2
Hardware Polisher	25
Tin-Plate Slitting Machine Operator	24
Bread Wrapping Machine Operator	23.6
Foundry Molder	23.3
Warehouse Order Picker	23
Broom Assembly Line Operator	20
Automatic Punch Press Operator	19.2
Bottling Line Operator	19
Tin-Plate Paint Drying Line Unloader	17.4
Automatic Brush Twisting Machine Operator	17.3
Heavy Hydraulic Press Operator	17
Washing Machine Wringer Assembly Line Operator	15
Automatic Washing Machine Assembly Line Operator	14.8
Plastic Injection Molding Machine Operator	12.8

Organization of This Report

In this chapter we have tried to set the stage for the presentation of findings which follows. Chapter 2 deals with the relationship we discovered between the task attributes and attendance. The reader will see how we found that the higher scoring tasks were associated with relatively high attendance. Chapter 3 is the story of our attempt to find a similar relationship between task attributes and job satisfaction as measured by the questionnaire. Chapter 4 tells how, when we divided our sample into two subpopulations based on subcultural predispositions, we found two different relationships between task attributes and satisfaction. Various explanations for this unexpected difference in response by workers in "Town" and "City" settings are discussed in Chapter 5. Finally, Chapter 6 summarizes the findings of the study and how they could be implemented both in practice and in future research.

CHAPTER 2

Task Attributes and Attendance

As HAS ALREADY been explained, a major hypothesis of this study was that our measurements of task attributes would be positively related to workers' attendance measured in terms of frequency of reported absence. More specifically, we hypothesized that high scores on the Requisite Task Attribute Index would be associated with high Attendance (infrequent absence), and low RTA scores with low Attendance, for those workers (403 out of the total sample of 470) for whom absence records were available. The first section of this chapter presents the evidence which confirmed this hypothesis. The discovery of an over-all relationship between the RTA Index and Attendance raised two further questions on which data will be presented in this chapter:

1. How was Attendance related to some of the more detailed measures of the nature of the task, namely, the major components of the RTA Index and certain Associated Task Attributes?
2. How was the relationship between the RTA Index and Attendance influenced by certain individual and situational factors which might be considered as supplementary variables with an "intervening" influence between our major job attribute and response variables?

A consideration of these questions, particularly the manner in which the over-all relationship was present for various subpopulations of the total sample, may help to explain what Attendance as a measure of response to the nature of the work really means. Then in the following chapter we will examine in detail the relationship between task attributes and job satisfaction.

The Over-All Relationship

The RTA Index scores were significantly related to the number of reported times absence during the previous 12 months. Jobs that scored high on the RTA Index were associated with good attendance (infrequent absences) ; low scoring jobs with poor attendance. To this extent, our general hypothesis that an independent measure of the technologically determined attributes of a job would predict worker response was confirmed. The greater the number of prescribed and discretionary activities and interactions, and the more knowledge, skill, and sense of responsibility intrinsic to the work, the more likely was worker response to be characterized by very low absenteeism, suggesting a favorable kind of involvement in the task.

A somewhat detailed picture of how Attendance was associated with the task is presented in Exhibit 2.1, which shows the number of men in each of seven attendance categories who were on jobs with high, medium, or low RTA Index scores.[1] In the last row of the exhibit are the total numbers of workers in each attendance category. It can be seen that most workers had very good attendance records; almost half of the 403 whose records were available had less than two absences. The numbers in parentheses in the exhibit show the approximate percentages of the totals in each attendance category who were on high, medium, or low scoring tasks. An examination of these percentages shows the extent to which workers with frequent absences (low attendance) are more likely to be found on low scoring jobs than workers with infrequent absences. For example, 49% of the men with six through nine absences had low RTA jobs, whereas 53% of those with one absence had high RTA jobs.

---

[1] The three categories (high, medium, and low) of RTA Index scores were established so as to be roughly equal for the total population. However, as seen in Exhibit 2.1, most workers for whom attendance records were *not* available were on medium and, especially, low RTA jobs.

Exhibit 2.1

NUMBER OF ABSENCES IN RELATION TO REQUISITE TASK ATTRIBUTE INDEX
(403 Workers)

RTA Index	No available absence data	Number of Recorded Absences in Previous 12 Months							Totals for whom absence data were available
		0	1	2	3	4–5	6–9	10+	
High	2 (3%)	43 (40%)	48 (53%)	20 (38%)	9 (22%)	10 (23%)	7 (20%)	10 (31%)	147 (36%)
Medium	25 (37%)	37 (34%)	23 (25%)	22 (41%)	16 (39%)	17 (40%)	11 (31%)	13 (41%)	139 (35%)
Low	40 (60%)	28 (26%)	20 (22%)	11 (21%)	16 (39%)	16 (37%)	17 (49%)	9 (28%)	117 (29%)
Totals	67	108	91	53	41	43	35	32	403

Exhibit 2.2

(403 Workers)

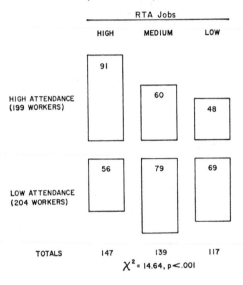

$\chi^2 = 14.64, p < .001$

The over-all association between Attendance and the RTA Index is presented more clearly in Exhibit 2.2; the 403 workers with available absence records are divided into six categories formed by the intersection of high, medium, and low RTA Index scores with *two* attendance categories, "high" (under two absences) and "low" (two or more absences). As the exhibit shows, 91 of 147 men with high tasks (62%) had high attendance, whereas 69 of 117 with low tasks (59%) had low attendance records. According to the Chi Square test of significance, the association indicated by the exhibit between task and attendance has a probability of less than .001 of occurring by chance.[2]

[2] As mentioned earlier, the Chi Square test will be our principal means for indicating the significance of the association between two variables. By itself this test says nothing about the particular pattern or directionality of the association. The bar-graph type of presentation in Exhibit 2.2 and subsequent exhibits, and the percentages in the text, are given to help the reader

Exhibit 2.3

REQUISITE TASK ATTRIBUTE INDEX IN RELATION TO ATTENDANCE:
EIGHT RTA CATEGORIES
(470 Workers)

RTA Index Scores	High Attendance Records	Low Attendance Records	Attendance Records Not Available	Totals
Highest 8	37	24	0	61
7	31	16	1	48
6	37	20	3	60
5	38	53	13	104
4	13	27	10	50
3	24	33	30	87
2	10	20	10	40
Lowest 1	9	11	0	20
Total	199	204	67	470

Exhibit 2.3 shows the same relationship except that the RTA Index scores are placed in eight categories from highest to lowest. (The numbers in each of the eight task categories for whom no attendance records were available are also indicated.) This exhibit shows that the majority of the men in the highest three task categories were absent less than two times, whereas attendance was consistently less regular in the lowest five RTA categories. The exhibit indicates a rather remarkably consistent relationship, and makes it seem unlikely that this finding has been artificially produced by uneven distribution over the RTA Index of the men for whom attendance records were not available.

The Separate Task Attributes and Attendance

The association between Attendance and the major task attributes is summarized in Exhibit 2.4, which shows a consistent tendency for workers with high attendance records to

visualize the *manner* in which the two variables are related to each other. In commenting on subsequent Chi Square tests, we will use the term "significant" for any association which has a probability of less than .05 of occurring by chance.

Exhibit 2.4

MAJOR TASK ATTRIBUTES IN RELATION TO ATTENDANCE
(403 Workers)

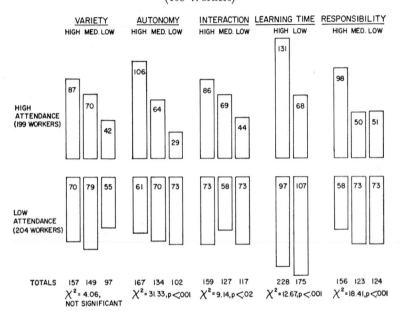

be on jobs with high task attribute scores.[3]   The association is especially strong in the case of Autonomy, Responsibility, and Learning Time (our measure of requisite knowledge and skill).   This was an expected finding in that the task attributes, as has been explained, were selected as likely to influence worker response, and frequency of reported absence had been selected as one measure of response.   But we had no prior research or theory with which to predict *which* of the various attributes would be more or less strongly related to attendance, or what the more precise pattern of these predicted relationships might be.

In the case of Variety (prescribed activities) and Interac-

[3] A significant association (*p* less than .001) between high and low attendance scores and an over-all rating of similar job attributes had been found by Walker and Guest (1952), p. 120, Table 11.

tion, some of the individual components underlying the major attribute were more strongly related to attendance than the major attribute itself. The score for Variety, it may be remembered, was obtained by combining the scores for Object Variety (the number of objects, tools, and controls which an individual was required to use on his job) and Motor Variety (the amount of required change in work pace, physical location, and type of physical motion). Object Variety, as we measured it, was not related to attendance at all. On the other hand, the association between Motor Variety and Attendance was very strong. The majority of those men on jobs with medium and low Motor Variety were found to have poor attendance records, whereas the upper third on Motor Variety were much more likely to have good attendance (probability less than .001).

The Interaction measure in Exhibit 2.4 combines Required Interaction and Optional Interaction on and off the job. All of these individual interaction measures were significantly associated with Attendance.

As shown in Exhibit 2.4, Learning Time and Responsibility were also very strongly related to attendance records. All jobs were scored on a nine-point scale according to the amount of time, ranging from less than one week to over 32 months, which was required on the job, according to the best informed opinion of supervision, before an operator was able to perform all aspects of the work to acceptable standards. (This score corresponded very closely to the estimates of required learning time which workers themselves gave subsequently in their questionnaire responses.) About half the jobs studied had learning time of under two months, and, as shown in Exhibit 2.4, the 175 men on these jobs had significantly poorer attendance records than the 228 on jobs with longer learning times.

The pattern of the relationship shown by Exhibit 2.4 between Attendance and Responsibility is worth noting carefully. As can be seen, on jobs with medium responsibility scores, attendance was just as likely to be low as on jobs with low responsibility scores. The pattern of the relationship between attendance and two of the individual components of the responsibility index was especially interesting. These two components were Ambiguity of Remedial Action and Time Span of Discretion. For example, looking at the jobs at the extreme ends of the Remedial Action scale, of 78 men on jobs with the lowest ambiguity, 51 (65%) had more than two recorded absences; whereas only nine of the 32 men scored nine on Ambiguity of Remedial Action (28%) were absent that frequently. Time Span of Discretion was scored on a nine-point scale ranging from less than one-half a day to four months or more. However, Time Span turned out to be less than half a day for about one-half of the jobs, and the poor attendance records tended to be concentrated on these very low time-span jobs. When all jobs were divided into those with a time span of less than or more than one-half a day, the association with Attendance was highly significant (probability less than .001). It appears that the kind of involvement which creates very low absenteeism is not likely to occur on the large number of industrial jobs on which Time Span is less than half a day.

The major attribute with the most striking relationship to Attendance was Autonomy, our term for the amount of discretionary activity assumed by the job design. It will be recalled that the autonomy index was composed of five separate measures of the opportunity on a given job for the operator to exercise his own discretion or choice concerning: method, sequence, pace, quality of incoming materials, and outside services. Jobs scoring high on any of these aspects of autonomy almost inevitably scored high on all the others, although in particular instances one or another of the different kinds of autonomy would presumably have greater or lesser psychological importance. As can be seen in Exhibit 2.4, a clear majority of men on high autonomy jobs had high attendance, whereas 73 of 102 men with low autonomy had two or more absences with a probability of .001 of this degree of association occurring by chance. Clearly, the more discretion that an operator can exercise concerning how to do his job, the less likely he is to be frequently absent from work.

Associated Task Attributes

Tasks not only set up certain requisites for the behavior (Activity, Interaction, and Mental States) of people; they also have other attributes associated with them which we referred to in Chapter 1. Of particular interest at the moment is the associated attribute which we called Task Identity, and which was not included in the RTA Index in spite of the fact that our scores on Task Identity turned out to be strongly related to the other job attribute scores. The four aspects of task identity which we measured were: Clarity of Cycle Closure, Visibility of Transformation to the operator, Visibility in the Finished Product of this transformation, Magnitude of the Transformation in terms of value added by it. We believed that a relatively high score on all these measures would characterize a job with a clear-cut identity from a psychological standpoint, and that this clear identity would be associated with a more favorable response. However, the association between Attendance and Task Identity, while significant (probability less than .05), was not as strong as in the case of most of our requisite task attributes. The finding that there was a more favorable response, in terms of attendance, to complex task requisites than to high task identity, raises some interesting questions, because it might be argued that more complex tasks require a higher human "investment" of energy and psychic attention, while higher task identity would be more "rewarding." The relationship between investments and rewards in influencing response will be an underlying theme of the discussion in later chapters.

One other associated task attribute had a relationship to Attendance that is of interest, namely, Cycle Time. In one sense Cycle Time is a measure of repetitiveness; however, it was not included in the Variety Index, mostly because it was difficult to assign clear Cycle Times to several of the jobs, as explained in Chapter 1. Nevertheless, it was possible to assign a measure of Cycle Time to the jobs of 373 men for whom absence records were available. For these men, Cycle Time was found to be significantly associated with attendance when jobs with very short cycle times were separated from those with cycle times of three minutes or more. Ninety-two of 148 men (62%) on jobs with cycle times of less than three minutes had more than two recorded absences (probability less than .01).

Individual and Situational Variables

Having looked briefly at the relationship between Attendance and two of the more interesting associated task attributes, we return to the relationship between Attendance and the RTA Index, examining how this over-all relationship was influenced by the intervening effect of certain Individual Characteristics and Situational Factors. How these supplementary variables were related both to attendance and to the RTA Index is summarized in Exhibit 2.5. The purpose of examining these relationships is to see whether the over-all association between the RTA Index and Attendance can be accounted for by the intervening effect of any of these individual or situational variables.

As far as the individual characteristics were concerned, Education and F-scale scores, contrary to what might have been expected, were not significantly related either to the RTA Index or to Attendance. In other words, the high attendance response to high scoring tasks was apparently not caused, as might have been suspected, by better educated men with less frequent absences being found on the higher scoring jobs. In the case of Age and Seniority the situation is not so clear cut. In the first place, the majority of workers on higher scoring tasks were over 41 years of age (probability less than

Exhibit 2.5

THE RELATIONSHIP OF INDIVIDUAL CHARACTERISTICS AND SITUATIONAL FACTORS TO REQUISITE TASK ATTRIBUTE INDEX AND ATTENDANCE

Individual Characteristics	Association with RTA Index	Association with Attendance
Education	Not significant	Not significant
F-Scale Score	Not significant	Not significant
Age	Positive ($p < .01$)	Positive ($p < .10$)
Seniority	Positive ($p < .001$)	Positive ($p < .05$)
Situational Factors		
Foreman Satisfaction	Negative ($p < .10$)	Not significant
Union Satisfaction	Negative ($p < .001$)	Not significant
Work Group Satisfaction	Not significant	Not significant
Company Satisfaction	Positive ($p < .05$)	Positive ($p < .05$)
Pay	Curvilinear ($p < .001$)	Negative ($p < .01$)

.01) and had 13 or more years of seniority (probability less than .001). Furthermore, there was a weak relationship between Age and Attendance, and a stronger relationship between Seniority and Attendance. This might imply that part of the over-all association between the RTA Index and Attendance was being caused by a tendency for men with longer seniority to have both high scoring jobs and relatively good attendance records. As a check of this interpretation, we tested the task-attendance relationship when Seniority was held relatively constant, by comparing high, medium, and low RTA scores with attendance separately for the 218 workers with 13 or more years of seniority and the 184 workers with less than 13 years of seniority. We found that for men with low seniority the association between RTA Index scores and Attendance remained significant, with high attendance on high scoring jobs (probability less than .01) and the association was in the same direction for the high seniority subpopulation, although not statistically significant. It seems safe to say, then, that the association between high task scores and good attendance in the population as a whole, while influenced by the relationship between both of these variables and seniority, was not merely a consequence of these relationships; attendance was related to the task regardless of seniority, but especially when seniority was low.

Turning now to the situational factors listed in Exhibit 2.5, it can be seen that satisfaction with the foreman, union, and work group was *not* acting as an intervening variable between RTA Index scores and Attendance. Attendance was not related to these satisfaction measures at all, and the association between RTA Index scores and Foreman Satisfaction and Union Satisfaction was negative. (These relationships are discussed in more detail in the next chapter.) It will also be noticed in Exhibit 2.5 that the direction of the relationship between Pay and Attendance was negative: attendance tended to be high when pay was low, whereas high pay was associated with poor attendance (probability less than

.01). The relationship between Pay and the RTA Index was strongly curvilinear (low pay associated with *medium* RTA scores). These findings concerning pay were intriguing and are discussed in subsequent chapters; for the present we need only to point out that they do not in themselves cast doubt on the RTA Index-Attendance relationship, since there seems to be no plausible way the two findings could be related.

Finally, Exhibit 2.5 shows that Company Satisfaction, like Seniority, has a significant positive relationship with both RTA scores and Attendance. That workers who are less frequently absent express more satisfaction with their company is not surprising, and confirms a similar finding among clerical workers in a large public utility.[4] The association between Company Satisfaction and both Attendance and the RTA Index suggests that company satisfaction might be creating the RTA Index-Attendance association. However, when RTA scores were held constant, there was no relationship between company satisfaction and attendance for either the high or medium group of RTA jobs. Only on the low RTA jobs was there a relationship between company satisfaction and attendance in the expected direction (probability less than .05). On the other hand, the relationship between the RTA Index and Attendance held up fairly steadily while Company Satisfaction was being held constant (probability less than .20 for high company satisfaction and probability less than .01 for low company satisfaction). The relationship between Company Satisfaction and the RTA Index will be examined in more detail in the next chapter.

Before leaving Exhibit 2.5, we should point out that the lack of significant relationship between Attendance and such situational factors as Foreman Satisfaction, Union Satisfaction, and Work Group Satisfaction is somewhat surprising. Other studies of attendance have usually indicated a positive association between attendance in various measures of both

[4] Mann and Baumgartel (1953). See also Kilbridge (1961b).

foreman satisfaction and work group cohesion.[5] Our findings served to raise questions of the generality of the earlier
research, but the present study was not designed to pursue
this question in depth.

Summary

The finding that the Requisite Task Attribute Index has
a strong influence on employee attendance records holds even
after detailed scrutiny. The evidence indicates that job design has a stronger influence on attendance than any of the
other variables discussed in this chapter. This includes both
the individual characteristics (education, F-scale, age, and
seniority) and the situational variable measures (foreman
satisfaction, union satisfaction, work group satisfaction, and
pay). The significant relationship between company satisfaction and attendance seemed to be primarily a result of the
association between Company Satisfaction and the RTA
Index. It was also found that of the major attributes making
up the RTA Index, Autonomy and Responsibility had the
strongest relationship with attendance. In total these findings give strong support to one of the researchers' initial
hypotheses, that attendance, as a direct behavioral measurement of a worker's involvement in his work, would vary
positively with the attributes of the work. In the next chapter we examine the relationship between the RTA Index and
our other major dependent variable, Job Satisfaction.

[5] These studies have almost always been confined to a single company; for
example, Mann and Baumgartel (1953). See also Hill and Trist (1962).

CHAPTER 3

Task Attributes and Job Satisfaction

THE PREVIOUS chapter has shown that technologically determined attributes of the job were significantly related to
workers' behavioral response to work: When the task was
relatively "complex" (high RTA scores) they were likely to
have nearly perfect attendance records; when the task was
relatively "simple" (low RTA scores) they were more likely
to be absent more frequently. But what was their *attitudinal*
response? Good attendance does not necessarily imply favorable attitudes. For example, in some cases the nature of a
particular technology might influence or coerce workers to
be very seldom absent from work which they actively dislike.
In this chapter we turn to our questionnaire data in order to
discover whether our ratings of task attributes were associated
with workers' expressed attitudes. More specifically, we are
concerned with the hypothesis that high scores on the RTA
Index would be positively associated with satisfaction with
the job as measured by questionnaire responses.

The principal response measure used for this purpose was
an index formed by combining scores on the first five items
in the questionnaire. As can be seen in Appendix A, these
questions all attempted to measure over-all satisfaction with
the job. When this measure of Job Satisfaction was cross-
tabulated with RTA Index scores, the major hypothesis just
referred to was not confirmed. There was no significant association between Job Satisfaction and RTA Index scores. As
Exhibit 3.1 indicates, when the jobs studied were divided
into eight steps from high to low scores on the RTA Index,

Exhibit 3.1

JOB SATISFACTION IN RELATION TO REQUISITE TASK
ATTRIBUTE INDEX
(470 Workers)

RTA Index Scores	Workers with High Job Satisfaction	Workers with Low Job Satisfaction	Total
Highest 8	37	24	61
7	23	25	48
6	32	28	60
5	52	52	104
4	24	26	50
3	46	41	87
2	18	22	40
Lowest 1	10	10	20
Total	242	228	470

the number of workers responding with high and low Job
Satisfaction was remarkably equal for each step.[1]

This chapter reports our attempts to understand in more
detail this lack of any over-all relationship between our requisite task and job satisfaction measures. First we present the
associations which were significant between Job Satisfaction
and the separate requisite task attributes. Next we examine
how Job Satisfaction and the RTA Index were both related
to the manner in which workers themselves perceived their
task attributes. We then present our attempt to discover
whether the RTA Index was related to Job Satisfaction for
certain subpopulations based upon individual characteristics
and attitudes toward various situational factors. Finally we
search the associations directly between the RTA Index and
workers' expressed satisfaction with various "situational"
factors for further clues about the impact of task characteristics on workers' attitudes. In Chapter 4 we describe the significant association between Job Satisfaction and RTA Index

[1] The same lack of association between the RTA Index and Job Satisfaction existed when the men for whom no attendance records were available
were eliminated from the sample.

scores which was finally discovered only when we divided the total population into two cultural categories which we call "Town" and "City."

The Separate Task Attributes and Satisfaction

Although the researchers found no significant relationship between the over-all RTA Index and Job Satisfaction, we speculated that some of the separate components of the Index might be associated with Job Satisfaction. However, in the case of most of the separate task attributes, our measures of job design appeared to be almost totally unrelated to Job Satisfaction scores, as far as the total survey population was concerned. Exhibit 3.2 summarizes the associations we discovered between the various job attributes and Job Satisfaction. Those attributes with a significant relation to Job Satisfaction are commented on below.

Exhibit 3.2

SEPARATE TASK ATTRIBUTES AND JOB SATISFACTION

Task Attributes	*Association with Job Satisfaction*
Variety Index	Not significant
Object Variety	Not significant
Motor Variety	Not significant
Autonomy Index	Not significant (Positive tendency)
Interaction Index	Not significant
Required Interaction	Not significant (Positive tendency)
Optional Interaction On-the-Job	Not significant (Positive tendency)
Optional Interaction Off-the-Job	Positive ($p < .01$)
Learning Time	Positive ($p < .05$)
Responsibility Index	Curvilinear ($p < .10$)
Ambiguity of Remedial Action	Not significant
Time Span of Discretion	Positive ($p < .001$)
Probability of Serious Error	Not significant
Task Identity	Not significant
Cycle Time	Not significant

When Optional Interaction Off-the-Job was split into high and low segments, the association with Job Satisfaction was significant at a probability level of .01. The pattern of this relationship when off-the-job time was broken down into four categories is indicated in Exhibit 3.3. The exhibit shows

Exhibit 3.3

OPTIONAL INTERACTION OFF-THE-JOB AND JOB SATISFACTION
(470 Workers)

Optional Interaction	*Job Satisfaction*			
	High		*Low*	
	No.	Per Cent	No.	Per Cent
Of 81 with 25% or More Off-the-Job Time	53	65%	28	35%
Of 89 with 10% to 25% Off-the-Job Time	49	55	40	45
Of 219 with zero to 10% Off-the-Job Time	110	50	109	50
Of 81 with No Off-the-Job Time	30	37	51	63

$$\chi^2 = 13.67, \; p < .01$$

that satisfaction was much more frequently expressed on jobs with 25% or more of off-the-job time. Furthermore, the majority was low satisfied only on those jobs on which Optional Interaction Off-the-Job was nonexistent. Apparently the amount of time available to leave the work-place temporarily is a source of satisfaction for workers who in other respects do not respond positively to high-scoring task attributes. However, high satisfaction with the opportunity to leave the job temporarily is not necessarily any evidence for a favorable response to complex work.

It will be remembered that we used the amount of time necessary to learn to perform the job satisfactorily as our measure of the knowledge and skill prescribed by the job design. In the previous chapter we reported a significant association between Attendance and Learning Time, when workers were divided into those on jobs with learning times of over and under two months. These particular Learning Time categories turned out *not* to be associated with Job Satisfaction. (Learning times of two to four months were very strongly associated with low rather than with high satisfaction.) However, when four months rather than two months was used as the division between high and low Learning Time, a significant association with Job Satisfaction appeared ($p < .05$). A majority of workers with learning times of four months or over had high Job Satisfaction, whereas a majority of those with shorter learning time had low Job Satisfaction.

The association between Job Satisfaction and the Responsibility Index is summarized in Exhibit 3.4. As indicated here, workers on jobs with medium responsibility scores were more likely to express low satisfaction; both high and low responsibility jobs on the other hand were more likely to be associated

Exhibit 3.4

RESPONSIBILITY INDEX IN RELATION TO JOB SATISFACTION
(470 Workers)

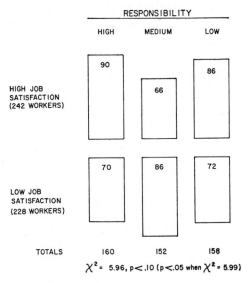

$\chi^2 = 5.96$, $p < .10$ ($p < .05$ when $\chi^2 = 5.99$)

with high satisfaction. This moderate tendency for low satisfaction to be expressed with jobs in the middle responsibility
range appears to us important. Two possible explanations
can be suggested for this curvilinear relationship (and for a
similar one to be reported later in this chapter). When this
pattern first began to appear at an early stage of our analysis,[2]
we tended to interpret it as signifying a preference by our
total population for tasks which offered a clear-cut way of
responding to work — with psychic involvement when the
task was complex, and with a simple exchange of time for pay
(low involvement with the task) on low content jobs.[3] We
hypothesized that this clarity would be preferred to the ambiguity inherent in middle level tasks, where some cues would
induce involvement and others indifference. As our analysis
proceeded further, however, we saw increasing evidence in
favor of a second interpretation, namely, that we were dealing
with two different working populations that brought some
different expectations or predispositions to the task. One
group found satisfaction on jobs with high complexity and
responsibility, whereas the other group was satisfied with
more simple, less demanding work. The mixing of two such
subpopulations could also account for the curvilinear response.

Examining in more detail the relationship between Responsibility and Job Satisfaction, the curvilinearity of this
association did not hold up in the case of two of the three
components of the Responsibility Index, Remedial Action

[2] In fact, a preliminary analysis for a portion of the total population dis-
played this same curvilinear relationship between Job Satisfaction and the
entire RTA Index.

[3] According to one writer: "There is no evidence that this worker attitude
is detrimental to his efficiency. . . . The worker sells his time and skill, a business transaction; the transaction complete, at quitting time he puts work out
of his mind. He is no longer the slave of a routine job, but has worked out
a sensible relationship with it. He is not bored with his job, he has come to
terms with it." (Anderson, 1961, p. xiii.) Of course, generalizations of this
kind have frequently been made, and our purpose in the present study was
to test their validity systematically.

and Time Span of Discretion. When these two variables were split into high, medium, and low categories, only Time Span showed a significant relationship with Job Satisfaction; low satisfaction was significantly associated with low (under one half-day) time span.

In short, we found a positive association between Job Satisfaction and Optional Interaction Off-the-Job, Learning Time, and Time Span of Discretion, and a curvilinear relationship with Responsibility. In general, the hypothesis that the requisite task would be positively related to Job Satisfaction was not confirmed. In the remaining pages of this chapter we will describe the results of some of our efforts to understand why Job Satisfaction was not more significantly related to task attributes. We will start by examining how both Job Satisfaction and the RTA Index were related to our measures of how workers perceived their jobs (Perceived Task Attributes).

Requisite and Perceived Task Attributes

The failure to discover an over-all significant relationship between requisite tasks and satisfaction raised the following questions:

1. Did workers perceive the attributes of their work differently from the way the researchers had scored the same attributes?
2. Did workers generally perceive their task in much the same way as the researchers had scored it but simply respond to it differently from what had been hypothesized, as far as the job satisfaction questions were concerned?

Included in the questionnaire were a number of questions concerning how workers themselves perceived the various task attributes which the researchers had scored. (See Questions 17–34, Appendix A.) Two indices were constructed from these questions. The Perceived Task Index (PT Index) was composed by combining relevant perceived task questions in a manner similar to the construction of the RTA

Index. The Perceived Opportunity to Contribute Index (**POC** Index) was constructed by combining those questions which emphasized primarily the worker's opinion as to whether or not he had an opportunity to contribute his skill and ideas usefully in accomplishing his assigned task.

Exhibit 3.5 shows the association between the Perceived Task Index and both the RTA Index and Job Satisfaction. It will be noted that workers on jobs with high RTA Index scores typically scored high also on the PT Index. The association was equally strong between RTA scores and POC. In this sense it can be said that in general workers "agreed"

Exhibit 3.5

REQUISITE TASK ATTRIBUTE INDEX AND JOB SATISFACTION
IN RELATION TO PERCEIVED TASK
(455 Workers)

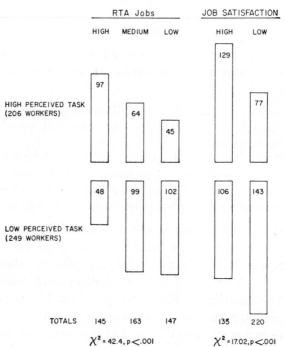

$\chi^2 = 42.4, p < .001$ $\chi^2 = 17.02, p < .001$

with the researchers concerning the attributes of their task, especially since responses to the separate perceived task questions, like the separate rated task attributes, were very strongly associated with each other. The association between perceived task scores and Job Satisfaction was virtually as strong as their association with the RTA Index. In the case of POC, the relationship with Job Satisfaction was even stronger. ($\chi^2 = 54.4$ $p < .001$) For example, almost twice as many workers with high Job Satisfaction also scored high instead of low on POC, whereas almost 70% of the 226 men with low Job Satisfaction perceived their job as being low on Perceived Opportunity to Contribute.

These very strong associations between our perceived task measures with both the RTA Index and Job Satisfaction seem to indicate that the perceived indices were a kind of link between the two otherwise unrelated general variables. Of course, to some extent the strong relationship between Job Satisfaction and perceived task measures can be explained by a general covariance tendency among questionnaire response items. In other words, there seemed to be quite a large number of workers who tended to answer all questions in a "favorable" manner and others for whom an "unfavorable" response was typical, regardless of the particular questionnaire item.

The possibility that the strong association between Job Satisfaction and perceived task measures was in part due to a "halo effect" or "acquiescence set" is also strengthened when we consider the relationship between perceived task and Attendance. In spite of the fact that Attendance was strongly related to the RTA Index, there was no significant relationship between Attendance and the Perceived Task Index. There was only a weak relationship between Attendance and Perceived Opportunity to Contribute (probability less than .10). Nevertheless, in spite of the difficulties of interpreting the significance of the results summarized in Exhibit 3.5, the strength of these associations strongly indicates that our task

ratings were relevant to workers' perceptions of the job, and
that the relationship between the RTA Index and Job Satisfaction merits further study. We turn next to examine how
these two major variables were related to each other for certain subpopulations.

Requisite Task and Job Satisfaction by Subpopulations

In the preceding chapter we analyzed the entire set of
situational factors and of individual characteristics to see if
the association between the RTA Index and Attendance
might be an accident of stronger associations with some of
these supplementary variables. We will now look at these
same two sets of variables but with a different question in
mind. Would dividing the total population into subpopulations in terms of these supplementary variables reveal a significant association between the RTA Index and Job Satisfaction that would otherwise be masked? For example, workers
with favorable attitudes toward their foreman or toward the
union might tend significantly to be satisfied (or dissatisfied)
with a certain kind of task, whereas workers with different attitudes toward foreman or union might have a different Job
Satisfaction response to the same kind of task.

When the five situational factors were used to subdivide the
total population, we discovered no hidden association between Job Satisfaction and the RTA Index. For example,
214 men scored "high" on Union Satisfaction. When the
relationship between the RTA Index and Job Satisfaction
was examined for this subpopulation, no significant association was discovered. In the same way there was no significant
association between task and Job Satisfaction for the 208
men who scored low on Union Satisfaction. Subpopulations
were also formed of those with favorable and with unfavorable attitudes toward the foreman, the company as a whole,
and their immediate work group. Job Satisfaction was not
related to the RTA Index for any of these subpopulations.
Another situational variable which might mask the relation-

ship between task and Job Satisfaction was Pay, but once again no relation appeared when Pay was held constant. We also dichotomized our population according to the size of the company, but again task and satisfaction were unrelated whether company size was large or small.

In looking for a supplementary variable which might explain how, if at all, Job Satisfaction and Requisite Task were related to each other, we also turned to our availible data on individual background factors. In the case of Education, this search also failed to produce significant results. Level of Education was related neither to the RTA Index nor to Job Satisfaction, and no relationship between task and satisfaction was discovered for either high or low education subpopulations.

In the case of the F-scale measure, there was some relationship with Job Satisfaction. Men scoring high on the F-scale were somewhat more likely to express high Job Satisfaction than those with low F-scale scores $(p < .05)$; however, F-scale was not associated with the RTA Index. One of our early hypotheses was that the F-scale results would help to interpret the relationship between task and Job Satisfaction in the following manner: It was thought that men with high F-scale scores would tend to express high satisfaction with low RTA jobs, and vice versa. (This hypothesis was strengthened by the preliminary results from the pilot study.) However, the F-scale scores completely failed to discriminate in this manner two different satisfaction responses to the Requisite Task. In fact there were no significant associations in either direction between task and satisfaction, whether F-scale scores were high or low.

The two remaining individual characteristics to be considered in this manner were Age and Seniority. About half the population about whom age data were available were over 41 years old. These older men were significantly more likely to have high Job Satisfaction than those of age 40 and under $(p < .02)$. However, Age was no more effective than

F-scale or Education in producing two subpopulations with a different satisfaction response to Requisite Task. For both the older and the younger group, Job Satisfaction and the RTA Index showed no significant association.

Seniority, which of course was closely related to Age, showed a somewhat similar pattern as far as the association with both Job Satisfaction and Requisite Task was concerned. As shown in Exhibit 3.6 there was a tendency for high seniority to be associated with high Job Satisfaction, although this tendency was not statistically significant except

Exhibit 3.6

JOB SATISFACTION AND REQUISITE TASK ATTRIBUTE INDEX
IN RELATION TO SENIORITY
(465 Workers)

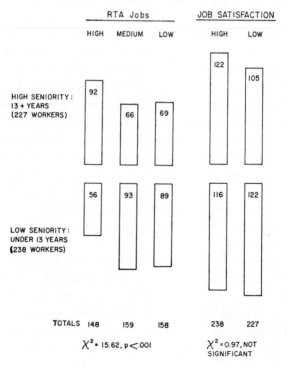

	RTA Jobs			JOB SATISFACTION	
	HIGH	MEDIUM	LOW	HIGH	LOW
HIGH SENIORITY: 13 + YEARS (227 WORKERS)	92	66	69	122	105
LOW SENIORITY: UNDER 13 YEARS (238 WORKERS)	56	93	89	116	122
TOTALS	148	159	158	238	227

$\chi^2 = 15.62, p < .001$ $\chi^2 = 0.97$, NOT SIGNIFICANT

in the case of men on high RTA jobs. In other words, only for the third of the population with high RTA jobs were men with high seniority significantly likely to have higher Job Satisfaction than men with low seniority. In addition, and as reported in Chapter 2, Seniority was related to RTA scores. As Exhibit 3.6 shows, 92 (62%) of those on high RTA jobs had high seniority, whereas the majority of those on medium and low RTA jobs had low seniority, indicating some tendency for more experience to be required or for less turnover to be caused by high-rated than by low-rated tasks. When the relationship between Job Satisfaction and the RTA Index was examined separately for those with high and with low seniority, the results were more suggestive than in the case of other individual background factors, although still not significant in a statistical sense. There were 92 men with high seniority on high RTA jobs, of whom 56 expressed high Job Satisfaction, and the response to medium and low RTA jobs was about equally divided between high and low Job Satisfaction for high seniority men. On the other hand, men with low seniority were somewhat more likely to express low Job Satisfaction with high RTA jobs. In other words, by dividing

Exhibit 3.6A

JOB SATISFACTION IN RELATION TO HIGH REQUISITE TASK
ATTRIBUTE INDEX AND SENIORITY

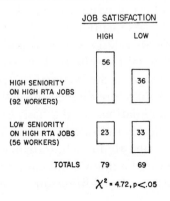

the total population into two groups with high and low seniority, it was possible to discern two contradictory tendencies which for the total population were canceling each other out. Furthermore we can achieve somewhat more statistical respectability for this finding by concentrating on the following question: What was the response in terms of Job Satisfaction to work scored high on the RTA Index? As shown in Exhibit 3.6A, the response of high seniority men to high RTA Jobs tended to be high Job Satisfaction and the response of low seniority men to high RTA Jobs tended to be low Job Satisfaction, with a probability of less than .05 of this degree of association between Seniority and Job Satisfaction on high RTA jobs occurring by chance.

However, this attempt to use Seniority as a relevant intervening variable between Requisite Task and Job Satisfaction is not entirely satisfactory, partly because the result is less clear cut when the response to medium and low RTA jobs is considered, and partly because there is no very convincing theory to explain the more favorable response of high than of low seniority men to high RTA jobs, although the result does seem quite reasonable once one has discovered it.

A final attempt to discover an individual characteristic with a significant "intervening" effect on the relationship between task and satisfaction should be reported. For reasons that are discussed more fully in the following chapter, we became interested in the effect of religious and ethnic background on response to work. (As mentioned in Chapter 1, the possible influence of ethnic or religious background on response was not part of the original hypothesis of the study, but emerged in the course of analyzing the material presented in the present chapter.) We therefore divided the 470 men in the sample into two subpopulations on the basis of their surnames: 245 whose names clearly indicated an ethnic origin usually regarded as Catholic (mostly French, Italian, or Irish) and 189 whose names indicated a non-Catholic origin (English, Scandinavian, or Jewish). In addition there were a small number (36) whose surnames were unknown. However, no significant association between RTA Index scores and Job Satisfaction was discovered for either subpopulation formed in this way. Ethnic or religious background, as an *individual* characteristic, showed no systematic influence upon whether response to task complexity was favorable or not in terms of expressed satisfaction. It was only when the influence of ethnicity and religion was considered in terms of varying subcultural patterns on a plant-by-plant basis that we finally discovered the two subpopulations we were looking for with contrasting responses to task attributes. This step is described in the following chapter.

Requisite Task and Satisfaction with Situational Factors

Since we failed to find a significant over-all association between the RTA Index and Job Satisfaction, we undertook a somewhat detailed examination of the relationship between the Requisite Task and our measures of the workers' satisfaction with other situational factors. This was done in a search for leads to further understanding of the way workers were responding to the nature of their tasks. Only those findings that were helpful as leads will be reported below.

The Company Satisfaction Index was composed of five general questions on the desirability of the company as a place to work. For most men in the sample, responses to these questions were very similar to the responses to the five questions on which the Job Satisfaction Index was based; the two indices were very strongly associated with each other. However, Company Satisfaction turned out to have a more significant relationship to the Requisite Task then did Job Satisfaction. Company Satisfaction tended to be high when the RTA Index was either high or low, whereas 60% of the workers on medium rated tasks expressed low Company Satisfaction. ($\chi^2 = 9.71$, $p < .01$) This was similar to the pattern which was recorded earlier (Exhibit 3.4) between Job Satisfaction and the Responsibility Index; a relatively unfavorable response associated with jobs in the middle range of our scales, and a favorable response associated with work which was either more complex or more simple than this middle range.

Of the major attributes of the RTA Index, both Autonomy and Interaction failed to show a significant association with Company Satisfaction. In the case of both Variety and Responsibility, however, the pattern was very similar to that existing between Company Satisfaction and the over-all RTA Index itself. About 60% of the men on jobs which scored in the middle range on these two measures had low Company Satisfaction, whereas majorities of those scoring high and low on both Variety and Responsibility expressed relatively high satisfaction with the company. Apparently two different patterns of response were present in our population. However, it was not clear why this pattern manifested itself in relation to Variety and Responsibility more than to the other job attributes, nor why it was significantly expressed in terms of satisfaction with the company rather than in terms of satisfaction with the job itself.

Work Group Satisfaction, like the other situational satisfaction measures, was significantly associated with Job Satisfaction. In fact, over two thirds of the men who were scored high on Job Satisfaction were also scored high on Work Group Satisfaction. This being the case, it was not surprising to discover no significant association between Work Group Satisfaction and the RTA Index. However, Work Group Satisfaction was strongly related to one important component of the RTA Index, Autonomy $(\chi^2 = 7.92, p < .02)$; and it was also significantly related to Task Identity $(\chi^2 = 7.47, p < .05)$ which it may be remembered was a job measure not included in the Requisite Task Index itself. Men whose jobs scored high on these two measures were significantly more likely to report high cohesion than those whose jobs scored low on the same measures. Interestingly, the tendency for a similar relationship between Work Group Satisfaction and Interaction, while present, was much less strong. Apparently, for our sample, frequency of contact with other men in the group was a less important source of a feeling of group cohesiveness than being on that sort of job where the task was clearly identifiable and the opportunity to exercise autonomy concerning the work was higher than usual.

Now we turn to Foreman Satisfaction and Union Satisfaction, two situational measures for which we found an association with Requisite Task in the opposite direction from that which might have been expected. In the case of Foreman Satisfaction the relationship with the RTA Index was not strong, but the majority of men on low RTA jobs expressed *high* satisfaction with their foremen. The tendency for low task to be associated with high Foreman Satisfaction was strongest in the case of Variety. Workers on high variety jobs were equally divided between high and low Foreman Satisfaction, but 59% of the workers on medium variety jobs expressed low Foreman Satisfaction, with the probability of this association occurring by chance being less than .02 $(\chi^2 = 8.25)$. Attitudes toward supervision were not a major focus of this study, but this tendency for men to be more satisfied with their foreman when their Task Variety is low than when it is medium or high deserves careful consideration in future studies. It might be thought that Foreman Satisfaction would be related to the task in much the same way as was the Work Group Satisfaction Index. This was not true for the separate attributes of the RTA Index, but it was moderately true in the case of Task Identity. A majority of the men on jobs with high and medium Task Identity expressed high Foreman Satisfaction, whereas low satisfaction with the foreman was more typical on jobs with low Task Identity $(\chi^2 = 5.34, p < .10)$. In other words, workers were more likely to be satisfied with their foreman when the identity of the task was clear and variety was low.

In the case of Union Satisfaction the tendency for a favorable response on low scoring jobs was very strong, as indicated in Exhibit 3.7. Two hundred fourteen of the 422 men who

Exhibit 3.7

REQUISITE TASK ATTRIBUTE INDEX, INTERACTION, AND
RESPONSIBILITY IN RELATION TO UNION HELPFULNESS
(422 Workers)

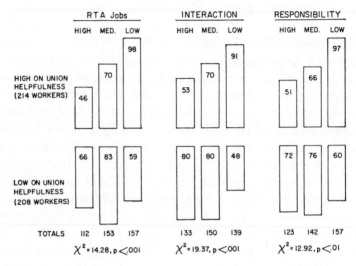

answered the question on the union[4] indicated the most
favorable alternative ("the union is very helpful"). These
214 workers were much more likely to have low RTA jobs
than those whose union attitudes were less favorable. This
association was caused primarily by a similar relationship between Union Satisfaction and Interaction and Responsibility.
Variety and Autonomy, and also Task Identity, were *not* significantly associated with Union Satisfaction. The very
strong negative relationship between attitudes toward the
union and sense of responsibility can most easily be interpreted by supposing that workers whose task requires or
expects little sense of responsibility compensate for this
fact by becoming favorably involved with the union and re-
garding it as "very helpful." A similar compensating mech-

[4] All but two of the 48 men who did not answer the question on Union
Satisfaction worked in the one company in our sample where there was no
union. It happened that none of these 48 men was on a low RTA job.

anism might be operating in the case of Interaction; however, we have no strong evidence to support this explanation nor can we easily explain why we did not discover a similar association between Union Satisfaction and Variety or Autonomy.

Summary

This chapter has been a report of our attempt to discover a meaningful relationship between the requisite attributes of work and the satisfaction workers express with their tasks. One could, of course, conclude that the lack of a clear-cut association for the total population between these two variables indicates quite simply that the nature of work has no measurable influence on workers' feelings of satisfaction with the job. However, before the researchers could convince themselves or anybody else of the validity of such a "no solution" finding, every avenue of inquiry needed to be pursued. And, as reported in this chapter, this pursuit only served to convince the researchers the more that, while their original hypothesis about an over-all relation was false, there still existed a more complex but systematic relation between these two key variables.

In this chapter we have found that there was a significant positive relation between Job Satisfaction and three requisite task attributes — Optional Interaction Off-the-Job, Learning Time, and Time Span of Discretion. These findings will need further testing because these particular attributes were not uniquely expected to relate to Job Satisfaction on the basis of any prior hypothesis.

We have also found that our two indices of Perceived Task Attributes relate to both the researcher-rated RTA Index and to Job Satisfaction. This finding suggests that some subpopulation of workers, unlike the majority, see their jobs as having higher attributes than the researchers and express high Job Satisfaction. Is there a subpopulation that is systematically distorting their perceptions of their jobs?

In searching among the various supplementary variables, both situational and individual, we found no way to subdivide our total population into groups responding in opposite ways to the nature of their tasks. The only variable of interest in this regard was Seniority. There was a tendency for high seniority people to find higher job satisfaction on higher rated tasks and vice versa, while the low seniority people expressed more job satisfaction on the low rated tasks. This is an example of the intervening effect we were searching for, but the tendency was not strong enough to rule out its being a chance finding.

In searching for other leads among the situational factors, we found an intriguing curvilinear relationship between Company Satisfaction and the RTA Index. This, in combination with the similar curvilinear relation between Responsibility and Job Satisfaction, again suggests the existence of two groups of workers, one that is attracted to high content work and the other that is attracted to low content work. A similar indication can be read into the discovery of a *negative* relationship between task attribute scores and satisfaction with both foreman and union.

In the next chapter we will report the discovery of two subpopulations of our sample that did have these distinctly opposite responses to the nature of their work. These subpopulations turned out to be workers from different subcultures of our total culture, who seem to bring to work quite different expectations or predispositions and accordingly respond quite differently to the same task. The researchers came to label these two groups "Town" and "City" workers. The next chapter explains the nature of these groups and their different responses to work.

CHAPTER 4

The Effect of Town and City Subcultures

IN CHAPTER 1, and again in Chapter 3, we have reported that two large subpopulations in our sample responded in opposite ways to task attribute scores, and that these two opposing tendencies were responsible for the lack of association between task and satisfaction for the population as a whole. These two subpopulations were not clearly delineated by any of the situational variables or individual background factors that have been examined in Chapter 3, such as attitude toward the union or F-scale scores or individual ethnicity as indicated by origin of surname. Rather the members of each of these subpopulations had in common the fact that they lived and worked in one of two readily identifiable cultural settings, to which we have given the labels "Town" and "City." The story of this chapter, in brief, is that we discovered a positive relationship between the RTA Index and Job Satisfaction (high task associated with high satisfaction) for the Town cultural setting, and a negative relationship between task and satisfaction for the City setting.

Town and City as Cultural Settings

In searching for a factor which would identify two possibly different response patterns to the nature of work, we were reminded of what has frequently been a hypothesis and occasionally a finding of other students of this subject, namely that the large urban cultural setting is associated with a different response to work than a rural or town environment. Frequently this rural-urban dichotomy is associated also with religion, in that the rural type of response to work is thought to be more closely related to the "Protestant ethic" whereas

69

the urban type of response is more likely to be identified with Catholicism.[1] It can be argued, for example, that a rural and Protestant upbringing tends to promote an attitude toward living in which involvement in work and the job are more highly valued than in a culture with less stress on individual achievement and more interest in social and political activity off the job.

The urban-rural and the religious differences are often talked about as though they identified one cultural dimension according to which workers' response to the task could be identified. Actually, of course, they are two separate dimensions which do not necessarily coincide. When we examined our population with these factors in mind, looking not at each individual but at each plant location and the nature of

[1] The identification of Protestantism with greater commitment to a work-oriented value system has been a well-known idea at least since the work of Weber (1958, originally published in 1904) and Tawney (1937). This notion implies that attitudes toward work and values in relation to it are essentially culturally determined, as Hearnshaw (1954) argued in an interesting cross-cultural survey of the problem. This area has recently become accessible to systematic research, thanks to McClelland's (1961) notable cross-cultural investigations of "achievement motivation." In a recent article Rosen (1959), making use of McClelland's methodology, has investigated similar differences identified with discrete ethnic-religious subcultures; we make use of Rosen's study in Chapter 5. Lenski's (1961) detailed study of the relationship between religious background and attitudes toward political and economic issues is equally relevant. Most interesting for our purposes is Lenski's finding (in a 1958 survey in the Detroit metropolitan area) that positive attitudes toward work are more frequent among upper-middle-class white Protestants and lower-working-class white Catholics, whereas negative attitudes toward work are more frequent among lower-working-class white Protestants and middle-class white Catholics (Lenski (1961), Table 10, p. 87). With the exception of Rosen's and Lenski's contributions, there has apparently been little systematic research on the effect of subcultural identifications on response to work, although a number of case studies have pointed in this direction. More specifically, our own attention to the difference that ethnic-religious and urban or rural background might make was suggested by several studies involving very small numbers of workers, such as the "prediction study" of our colleagues, Zaleznik, Christensen, and Roethlisberger (1958), the article by Whyte (1944) on attitudes toward unionism, and the characterization by Dalton (1948) of the nine outstanding "rate busters" in a department of 300. (See also Dalton, 1947, and Faunce, 1960).

the surrounding community from which it drew its work force, it was possible to identify quite clearly three different ethnic-religious cultural settings. Two hundred and two men in the sample belonged to a work force and lived in a community in which virtually every worker had an ethnic origin generally considered Catholic (French, Italian, and Irish). One hundred and sixty-one men worked and lived where almost everyone belonged to ethnic groups usually considered Protestant (English and Scandinavian, for example). One hundred and seven men were classified as "mixed" on the ethnic-religious dimension since the group with which they worked and lived could not be clearly identified as belonging to either of the preceding categories. By looking separately at the urban-rural dimension, it was found that 244 men in the sample worked in plants which were located in or near a large city where the working population almost all lived in a large urban community. Two hundred twenty-six men, on the other hand, worked in plants which were not located near a large city and which recruited their work force almost entirely from the surrounding farm country or small rural towns.

Exhibit 4.1

CULTURAL SETTINGS FOR 470 WORKERS

	Urban	*Rural*	*Total*
Protestant	0	161	161
Catholic	137	65	202
Mixed	107	0	107
Total	244	226	470

Exhibit 4.1 shows how these two dimensions interacted with each other for our sample. It will be noted that the 226 men in a rural setting included 65 who had been placed in the Catholic ethnic-religious group. We discovered that the response to the task of these 65 men was much more similar to the response of the others in rural settings than to the response of the other members of the Catholic ethnic-religious group.

On the other hand, the 244 men in the urban setting included 107 whose ethnic-religious background had been classified as mixed. We discovered that these 107 men showed no consistent pattern of response to Requisite Task Attributes. It was as though for them the subculture was too diffuse or disorganized to be exerting a strong influence on the manner in which they responded to work. In other words, out of the total sample we found 363 men who came from a fairly clearcut ethnic-religious cultural environment, and we divided these 363 men into two categories depending upon whether their cultural setting was primarily rural or urban. This gave us two categories: 137 City workers and 226 Town workers. The City category happens not to include anyone in the Protestant ethnic-religious group, and the Town category happens not to include any of the 107 whose ethnic-religious background was mixed. Because their response was not clear cut we will not include these 107 men in the following exhibits of this chapter, although we will be mentioning them in passing from time to time. (Another reason that this mixed group is not particularly relevant to our present purposes is that it happened that none of them were scored "high" on the RTA Index. This is why there will seem to be more than a normal number of men with high RTA scores in many of the following exhibits.)

Attendance and Cultural Setting

Although the main purpose of this chapter is to describe the relationship between Requisite Task Attributes and Job Satisfaction for the Town and City cultural settings, we shall first examine the effect of cultural setting on the relationship described in Chapter 2, namely that between the RTA Index and Attendance. The cultural setting was strongly associated with both Requisite Task Attributes and with Attendance. Town workers were much more likely than City workers to be on high scoring tasks ($\chi^2 = 25.8$, $p < .001$); Town workers were also more likely than City workers to have high Attendance $(\chi^2 = 5.81, p < .02)$. Association between Task and Attendance for Town workers was very strong $(\chi^2 = 20.7, p < .001)$. An examination of the same relationship for City workers showed no significant association between Task and Attendance, and no consistent directionality in the relationship. In other words, the significant association between Task and Attendance for the total population is a consequence of a very strong relationship between them for Town workers, which was not reversed by the City workers' response. Clearly these two settings were associated with two different responses to work as measured by Attendance; now we are ready to examine in some detail the nature of these differences when the response was measured in terms of Job Satisfaction.

Job Satisfaction and Cultural Setting

Unlike Attendance, Job Satisfaction was not related to cultural setting. Town and City workers were equally likely to express high or low satisfaction. However, the response to the task as measured by our Job Satisfaction Index was very different in these two cultural settings, as shown in Exhibit 4.2. For Town workers there was a moderate tendency for high satisfaction to be associated with high scores on the RTA Index, and for low satisfaction with low working tasks. Although there were only 41 Town workers with low RTA scores, 25 (61%) scored low on Job Satisfaction. In the case of City workers the association between Job Satisfaction and Task was in the opposite direction. Forty of the 58 City men with low Requisite Task Attributes (69%) had high Job Satisfaction scores, whereas low Job Satisfaction was the majority response of City men to both high and medium scoring tasks. This tendency for City workers to express high satisfaction with low scoring tasks and low satisfaction with high or medium tasks is sufficiently strong to have a probability of appearing by chance of less than .01 according to the Chi Square test. For the 108 men in the "mixed" cultural setting, there was no significant association between Requisite Task

Exhibit 4.2

Requisite Task Attribute Index in Relation to
Job Satisfaction for Town and City Workers
(363 Workers)

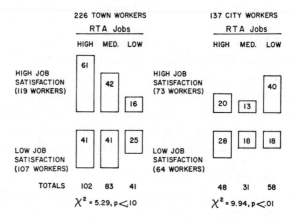

$\chi^2 = 5.29, p < .10$ $\chi^2 = 9.94, p < .01$

and Job Satisfaction. (It will be remembered that this group included no one with high RTA scores.) Consequently, when Job Satisfaction with high, medium, and low Requisite Task was summed for the three cultural settings, there was no significant association, as we already know, between the RTA Index and Job Satisfaction for the population as a whole.

The data in Exhibit 4.2 can be rearranged in order to examine the relationship between cultural setting and Job Satisfaction on jobs with high, medium, and low RTA scores. When Requisite Task scores were low, City workers had a strong tendency to express high satisfaction with their job, and Town workers a strong tendency to express low satisfaction with the same kind of work ($\chi^2 = 7.59$, $p < .01$). The opposite tendency on high scoring tasks was strong enough to approach statistical significance ($\chi^2 = 3.62$, $p < .10$). In short, and this is the central finding reported in this chapter, City workers responded with more satisfaction on low than on high scoring jobs, whereas Town workers were more frequently satisfied with high than with low scoring jobs.

Cultural Setting and Separate Task Attributes

In general, as would be expected, the cultural setting had an effect on the relationship between Job Satisfaction and the various components of the RTA Index which was quite similar to the effect upon the relationship between Job Satisfaction and the RTA Index itself. Exhibit 4.3 summarizes the associations we found in Town and City subpopulations between Job Satisfaction and the Requisite Task Attributes (and also the Associated Task Attributes, Cycle Time and Task Identity). The associations between the same variables for the total population, already reported in Chapter 3, are also indicated. The exhibit indicates the extent to which the various attributes separately contributed to the over-all tend-

Exhibit 4.3

ASSOCIATIONS BETWEEN JOB SATISFACTION AND TASK ATTRIBUTES
FOR TOWN AND CITY WORKERS

	Association with Job Satisfaction		
Task Attributes	*Town*	*City*	*Total Population*
Variety Index	+	−	0
Object Variety	+	0	0
Motor Variety	0	−	0
Autonomy Index	0	0	0
Interaction Index	+	0	0
Required Interaction	+	−	0
Optional Interaction On-the-Job	0	0	0
Optional Interaction Off-the-Job	+	0	+
Learning Time	+	0	+
Responsibility Index	+	0	C
Ambiguity of Remedial Action	+	0	0
Time Span of Discretion	0	0	+
Probability of Serious Error	0	0	0
Cycle Time	+	0	0
Task Identity	0	0	0

0 = no significant relationship.
+ = positive relationship significant at $p < .05$ level.
− = negative relationship significant at $p < .05$ level.
C = curvilinear relationship significant at $p < .10$ level.

ency for Town workers to be satisfied with high scoring jobs and for City workers to be more satisfied with low scoring jobs. It can be seen that nine of 15 indicated attributes were positively associated with Job Satisfaction for Town workers, whereas there were three negative associations in the case of City workers. Furthermore, there are no negative Town associations, and no positive City associations. Clearly, the same results that we have reported for the RTA Index hold in general for the individual task attributes as well. The following paragraphs present more detail concerning the more interesting associations summarized in Exhibit 4.3.

The two cultural subgroups responded in two distinctly different ways to Variety. A majority of Town workers with high and medium variety jobs expressed high job satisfaction, while 63% of the 52 Town workers with low variety had low job satisfaction ($\chi^2 = 8.61$, $p < .02$). For City workers, on the other hand, job satisfaction tended to be low on high and medium variety jobs, while of 58 City workers with low variety, 69% had high job satisfaction.[2] An examination of the relationship between job satisfaction and the two components of the Variety Index gave the following results. Town workers were significantly more satisfied when Object Variety was high than when it was low ($p < .01$), but Motor Variety was not significantly associated with Job Satisfaction in Town settings. For City workers, there was a nonsignificant tendency in the direction of high satisfaction with low Object Variety, and a significant association ($p < .05$) between high Job Satisfaction and low Motor Variety. This tendency can best be explained in terms of Baldamus' concept of "Traction."[3] Low Motor Variety is more conducive to the feeling

---

[2] Other studies, already referred to, had discovered that a significant number of workers were relatively well satisfied with comparatively repetitive work. See, for example, Great Britain, Industrial Health (Fatigue) Research Board (1937) and (1938); Wyatt and Marriott (1956). Our data emphasize that satisfied adaptation to repetitiveness is very much more likely to appear among City than among Town workers.

[3] Baldamus (1951) and (1961); Turner and Miclette (1962).

of being pleasantly pulled along by the inherent rhythm of the task than is low Object Variety. And City workers, apparently, were more likely than Town workers to associate this experience with favorable response to our measure of Job Satisfaction.

In the case of the Interaction Index, the familiar tendency of Town workers to express high satisfaction with high rated jobs was significant at the .05 probability level, but the opposite tendency for City workers was not statistically significant. The three Interaction components, considered separately, behaved in different ways. In the case of Optional Interaction Off-the-Job, high scores were significantly associated with high satisfaction for Town workers ($p < .02$) and there was a nonsignificant tendency in the same direction for City workers as well. The fact that City as well as Town workers tended to prefer jobs with an opportunity for frequent off-the-job interaction explains why this was one of the few separate task attributes to be positively related to Job Satisfaction for the total population. On the other hand, the response to Required Interaction showed a particularly dramatic reversal between the two subpopulations. Ninety out of 119 Town workers with high Job Satisfaction (76%) were on jobs with high Required Interaction ($\chi^2 = 13.8$, $p < .001$), whereas 60 out of 73 high satisfied City workers (82%) had low Required Interaction ($\chi^2 = 9.74$, $p < .01$). A plausible explanation of this response by City workers is that their over-all attitude toward the task predisposed them to prefer jobs on which they were not frequently interrupted by interactions related to the work.

The data in regard to Learning Time showed that the positive association with Job Satisfaction for the total population was entirely accounted for by the response of Town workers. In fact, City workers showed a nonsignificant tendency to respond in the opposite direction.

An examination of the results for the two cultural settings also helped to explain the over-all curvilinear relationship which was discovered between Responsibility and Job Satisfaction. Town workers on low Responsibility jobs tended to be evenly split between high and low satisfaction, whereas City workers on similar jobs (of whom there were only 48) showed a slight tendency toward high satisfaction. Both Town and City tended to respond with low satisfaction to medium Responsibility, whereas Town (but not City) workers with high Responsibility were predominantly high satisfied. These results combined with no significant association for the "mixed" group produced the "curve" described in Chapter 3 for the total population.

As for the two Associated Task Attributes, Task Identity, contrary to our predictions, was not significantly related to Job Satisfaction for either subpopulation. On the other hand, Cycle Time showed a strong positive association with satisfaction for Town workers $(p < .01)$ and a weak negative association for City workers $(p < .20)$. Furthermore, City workers were significantly more likely than Town workers to express high Job Satisfaction when Cycle Time was relatively low (under 30 minutes).

Summarizing the Town and City Job Satisfaction response to individual task attributes reveals the following pattern. Town workers responded especially positively to high scores on Object Variety, Required Interaction, Learning Time, and Responsibility. This response is similar to that reported by Herzberg, Mausner, and Snyderman (1959), who found opportunity at work for achievement, responsibility, learning, and recognition to be the most important positive "motivators" in a sample of engineers and accountants. City workers, on the other hand, expressed high satisfaction on jobs with low scores on Motor Variety, Cycle Time, and Required Interaction, a response which is most easily explained by means of Baldamus' (1951, 1961) concept of "Traction." City workers, apparently, have a predisposition to respond favorably to relatively repetitive work when not too frequently interrupted by Required Interaction. In City settings, in other words, frequent required interactions seem to function as "distractions" to the mildly favorable "working mood" which Baldamus finds a frequent response to smoothly running repetitive work. To this extent our examination of the different Town and City responses to the separate task attributes is helpful in understanding the difference in response to the RTA Index as a whole.

Cultural Setting and Situational Factors

We turn now to the effect of cultural setting upon the relationship between Requisite Task Attributes and various Situational Factors. These relationships are summarized in Exhibit 4.4, which also shows the associations between the

Exhibit 4.4

ASSOCIATIONS BETWEEN REQUISITE TASK ATTRIBUTE INDEX AND SITUATIONAL FACTORS FOR TOWN AND CITY WORKERS

	Associations with RTA Index		
Situational Factors	*Town*	*City*	*Total Population*
Union Satisfaction	$+ (p < .05)$	$- (p < .001)$	$- (p < .10)$
Company Satisfaction	$+ (p < .02)$	$- (p < .02)$	Curve $(p < .01)$
Work Group Satisfaction	0	$- (p < .10)$	0
Foreman Satisfaction	0	$- (p < .01)$	$- (p < .10)$
Job Satisfaction	$+ (p < .10)$	$- (p < .01)$	0

$+ =$ Positive association.
$- =$ Negative association.
$0 =$ No significant association.

four Situational Factors and RTA for the total population which were presented in Chapter 3. (In addition, the Town, City, and Total Population associations between RTA and Job Satisfaction are given in the last line of Exhibit 4.4 for purposes of comparison.) It can be seen that in each case the results for the total population can be explained as the consequence of a combination of the different response patterns in the two cultural settings.

In the case of Union Satisfaction and Company Satisfaction, the effect of introducing the cultural setting variable was the same kind of reversal in response to the task that we discovered in the case of Job Satisfaction. Thirty-seven of 58 City workers on low scoring jobs (64%) described the union as helpful, while high and medium RTA Index scores were associated with low union helpfulness for City workers ($\chi^2 = 26.7, p < .001$). For Town workers, on the other hand, there was high Union Satisfaction on high RTA jobs and low Union Satisfaction on medium RTA jobs ($\chi^2 = 7.69$, $p < .05$). However, because this reversal in the dominant pattern on the part of Town workers was not very strong, and because it did not apply to those Town workers on low scoring jobs, the pattern for the population as a whole remains the same as for City workers: high Union Satisfaction when Requisite Task was low. The association between Union Satisfaction and cultural setting for men with high Requisite Task Attributes was especially interesting. When RTA was high, Town workers tended to score high on Union Satisfaction while 38 of 48 City workers with high RTA (79%) had low Union Satisfaction scores ($\chi^2 = 12.8, p < .001$). Does this mean that City workers tend to blame their union for whatever it is that they dislike about high Requisite Task, whereas Town workers tend to give the union credit for their more favorable response to more complex work? We cannot answer this question without more clinical data concerning the particular union relationships involved, but the suggestion does seem to deserve further study.

As far as Company Satisfaction is concerned, Exhibit 4.4 serves as a reminder that there was a curvilinear relationship for the total population, with low satisfaction with the company most frequently expressed by workers with medium RTA Index scores. The reason for this over-all result became somewhat clearer when we examined the Town and

City data separately, particularly inasmuch as there was absolutely no association between Company Satisfaction and Requisite Task for the "mixed" cultural group. Town workers who scored high on Company Satisfaction were most frequently on high scoring jobs $(x^2 = 7.84, p < .02)$, whereas City workers scoring high on Company Satisfaction most frequently had low Requisite Task Attributes $(x^2 = 9.10, p < .02)$; both Town and City workers scoring low on Company Satisfaction had medium Requisite Task scores more frequently than would be the case if the two variables were randomly related to each other. Naturally, then, for the population as a whole, Company Satisfaction tended to be high when Requisite Task was either high or low, and this was the consequence of the pattern with which we are now familiar: high satisfaction on high tasks in Town settings and low satisfaction by City workers with the same kind of work.

It is worth emphasizing that in both cultural settings the response to the task in terms of attitudes toward the union was very similar to the response in terms of attitudes toward the company, in spite of the rather common assumption that favorable attitudes toward one of these institutions imply unfavorable attitudes toward the other. In fact, of course, this assumption has frequently been disproved in survey research, most notably perhaps in Purcell's studies (1953, 1960) of "dual allegiance" to company and union in the meat packing industry. ·When the nature of the work is in line with the cultural set or motivational predisposition that workers bring to the job, both company and union seem to be given credit for this state of affairs; when there is dissatisfaction with the job, both company and union seem to be blamed. This suggests for unions as well as management a need to learn more about how workers respond to different kinds of jobs.

In the case of two other Situational Factors, cultural predispositions did not produce a reversal pattern similar to the ones we have been considering. Work Group Satisfaction was not related to RTA for Town workers and there was only a slight tendency $(p < .10)$ for it to be low on medium tasks for City workers, and somewhat more frequently high when Requisite Task was low.   In the case of Foreman Satisfaction the slight tendency in the total population for Foreman Satisfaction to be high on low Requisite Task jobs was entirely accounted for by a strong association $(p < .01)$ between high Foreman Satisfaction and low Requisite Task for City workers.   In short, in spite of differences between the response patterns in terms of the four Situational Factors — Union, Company, Work Group, and Foreman Satisfaction — the unexpectedly favorable response by City workers to low scoring requisite tasks remains the most notable feature of these results.

Before leaving the topic of cultural setting and Situational Factors, we need to consider the data we secured on rates of Pay.   Although, in our original scheme (see Exhibit 1.2) Pay was listed as a supplementary variable which might have an intervening effect on the relationship between Requisite Task Attributes and our major response variables, it was not taken up in this way in Chapter 3.   This was because the effect of Pay on our other measures can best be explained only when the influences of cultural setting are also taken into account.

This study was not designed initially to give much concentrated attention to monetary rewards — either the workers' response to pay, or the way it was associated with different kinds of jobs.   For the purposes of this study the researchers measured Pay by taking an average, over a period of several weeks, of the gross weekly dollar earnings (excluding any overtime pay) of each person in the study.   This figure did not, of course, try to assign a dollar figure to fringe benefits such as health insurance, pensions, or vacations, but a cursory examination satisfied us that these items were reasonably uniform across the sample.   We adjusted this average gross weekly pay figure for all Canadian jobs by the average pay differential between all Canadian and U. S. jobs studied.

The resulting revised pay figures were used for all subsequent analysis. We had expected that pay would vary with the complexity and responsibility involved in the work; in other words, that pay would be positively correlated with our RTA Index. We also expected that pay would be related positively to age, seniority, and education, and also to Job Satisfaction.

When all the jobs were split into high and low categories, however, with the same high-low split made at the median pay rate, the resulting table showed a *negative* relationship between the variables $(\chi^2 = 5.69,\ p < .02)$. To secure a more detailed look at these surprising data, Exhibit 4.5 pres-

Exhibit 4.5

PAY IN RELATION TO REQUISITE TASK ATTRIBUTE INDEX BY OCTILES

RTA Index by Octiles	High Pay	Low Pay	Total
Highest 8	33	28	61
7	19	29	48
6	43	16	59
5	26	76	102
4	16	34	50
3	40	47	87
2	35	5	40
Lowest 1	20	0	20
Totals	232	235	467

ents Pay as high or low for all jobs broken into eight categories from high to low on the RTA Index. This exhibit indicates clearly that the medium range jobs are receiving low pay relative to both the high and low jobs on the RTA Index. And when the RTA Index scores are divided into the three familiar high, medium, and low categories, the relationship between Requisite Task and Pay was clearly curvilinear: 68% of 162 workers on medium scoring jobs were in the low pay category, whereas pay was high for a majority of those with both low and high RTA scores.

This curvilinear relationship between Pay and Requisite

Task, which remained significant for both Town and City subpopulations, might suggest that a favorable response to high pay on low rated jobs was masking the predicted positive relationship between task and satisfaction for the total population.   In other words, Pay rather than cultural setting might be the relevant intervening variable, especially if, as would be expected, pay was higher in City settings. However, contrary to the usual findings, City workers in our sample had a mean pay virtually identical with that of Town workers.   In short, the pay data do not provide a simple explanation of the City-Town difference in response.

Furthermore, such an explanation assumes not only a curvilinear relationship between pay and task, but also a positive relationship between pay and satisfaction.   However, for the total population we found *no* significant association between Pay and Job Satisfaction when each of the variables was split at the median.   On the other hand, a significant association *did* appear when Pay was split between the lowest quartile and the three higher quartiles $(x^2 = 9.29, p < .01)$.   In other words, workers with really low pay did tend to express low satisfaction, but above the lowest pay quartile, increases in pay did not influence satisfaction.   But when we examined this relationship separately for Town and City workers, as in Exhibit 4.6, we found that it was caused by the response of Town workers, and that pay seemed to have little direct influence on Job Satisfaction for City workers at any point in the pay continuum.   Once again, then, we find an unexpected response in the City setting, for which our pay data do not supply a satisfactory explanation.

Cultural Setting and Individual Characteristics

The hypothesis that the two cultural settings we are concerned with in this chapter represent important differences in motivational predispositions to the task is strengthened by a consideration of how workers' individual characteristics (Age, Seniority, Education, and F-scale) were related to Job

Exhibit 4.6

JOB SATISFACTION IN RELATION TO PAY FOR TOWN AND
CITY WORKERS
(359 Workers)

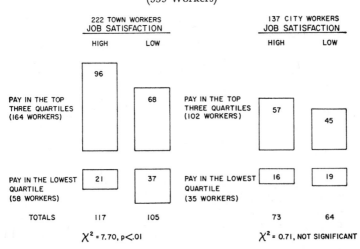

Satisfaction, RTA Index scores, and Pay.   Exhibit 4.7 summarizes the Chi Square associations between these variables, for the total population and separately for Town and City workers.   It can be seen that older and more senior Town workers had a significant tendency to express high job satisfaction, whereas for City workers high satisfaction was associated with low education and high F-scale.   There was an over-all tendency, with little significant distinction between Town and City, for older and better educated workers to be on high scoring tasks, as might be expected, but no association between F-scale and RTA Index scores.   However, Town workers with high seniority and education tended to receive relatively high pay, whereas for City workers high pay was associated with low age and seniority.

These results seem to us to imply some serious questions about the longer run consequences, for many workers, of the City type of adaptation to relatively simple tasks.   It would

Exhibit 4.7

ASSOCIATION BETWEEN INDIVIDUAL CHARACTERISTICS AND JOB
SATISFACTION, REQUISITE TASK ATTRIBUTE INDEX, AND PAY,
FOR TOWN AND CITY WORKERS

	Age	Seniority	Education	F-Scale
Job Satisfaction				
Town	+	+	0	0
City	0	0	—	+
Total	+	0	0	+
RTA Index				
Town	0	+	+	0
City	+	+	+	0
Total	+	+	0	0
Pay				
Town	0	+	+	+
City	—	—	0	0
Total	0	0	+	0

+ = Positive association, $p < .05$.
— = Negative association, $p < .05$.
0 = No significant association.

appear that, with increasing age and seniority, a worker who
at first expects little inherent interest or challenge in his job,
might become increasingly frustrated. As seniority increases
without any increase in knowledge and skill, it often appears
more and more difficult to leave undemanding work, especially when the pay is relatively high. Yet the costs in terms
of internal frustration and general bitterness can become very
great, a situation that was vividly illustrated in two previous
studies of older automobile assembly workers.[4]

A final point concerning these results of the effect of individual characteristics is the lack of association between task
attributes and F-scale scores, and the fact that F-scale and satisfaction were only related for City workers. Other studies,
for example the detailed work of Vroom (1960), have found
personality measures of this kind to be significantly related
to workers' response to their work experience. Our failure

[4] See Whyte (1961), pp. 179–197; and Turner (1955b) and Guest (1955b).

to find the F-scale a significant supplementary variable between task and response may have been caused by methodological difficulties. However, we believe the major reason was the overriding impact of subculturally determined predispositions.

In our attempt further to understand how cultural setting influenced worker response, we turn next to examine its effect on how workers in each setting perceived their task attributes, and how these perceptions were related both to Job Satisfaction and to the researchers' ratings of the same jobs. The purpose of this examination is to answer the question raised in Chapter 3 as to whether there was a subpopulation systematically "distorting" their perceptions of their jobs.

Cultural Setting and Perceived Attributes

It may be remembered that we used two main measures of the perception of their task attributes which workers expressed in their questionnaire: the Perceived Task Index (PT), a combination of all relevant questionnaire responses, and Perceived Opportunity to Contribute Index (POC), constructed of responses to questions concerning the extent that workers felt they could contribute their ideas and skills in accomplishing the task (see Appendix A for the construction of both these indices). When RTA, PT, and POC scores were split at their medians, almost all Town workers with high RTA Index scores had high PT and high POC. However, for City workers, the association between RTA and PT was less strong, and there was no significant association between RTA and POC. In short, the Town-City difference in response to work in terms of Job Satisfaction *was* partly caused by a difference in how the task was perceived in the two cultural settings. Town workers perceived their work much as the researchers did when they measured the various task attributes; City workers were more likely to differ in their perceptions, and in fact showed *no* tendency to perceive high opportunity to contribute on high scoring jobs.

A similar conclusion was warranted when RTA Index scores were divided into the familiar high, medium, and low categories. Most Town workers with high PT had high Requisite Task scores; the same tendency among City workers was not as strong. The difference between Town and City came out even more strongly in the association between high, medium, and low RTA Index scores and high or low POC. In the first place, Town workers were more likely to have high POC scores than were City workers; it will be remembered that they were also much more likely to be on high rated Requisite Task jobs, and rated and perceived measures were very strongly associated with each other. However, the relationship between POC and Requisite Task was not nearly as strong for City workers ($\chi^2 = 6.83$, $p < .05$) as for Town workers ($\chi^2 = 34.8$, $p < .001$). The difference between Town and City response to low Requisite Task was especially noticeable. Of 41 Town workers with low RTA, 30 (or 73%) had low POC, whereas a slight majority of City workers with low RTA had *high* POC. This association between POC and cultural setting on low RTA jobs was significant at the .01 probability level ($\chi^2 = 7.62$).

Apparently the generally favorable attitude of City workers to low scoring task attributes leads them to distort their perception of these tasks and to say that they have considerably more opportunity to contribute than they really do according to the researchers' ratings of these jobs. The perception of Town workers with low Requisite Task Attributes of their Opportunity to Contribute is significantly more in line with how the researchers scored their work. What are the causes and the consequences of this greater "distortion" by City workers in their perception of their jobs? Having expressed relatively frequent satisfaction with low-rated jobs, are they influenced by values prevalent in the larger society to see more opportunity to contribute than "really" exists? Or is the causation the other way; subcultural norms define more opportunity to contribute than Town workers see in similar work, and this greater perceived opportunity causes higher satisfaction? In any case, what does this greater "distortion" do to the way a City worker conceives of himself and his role; does it affect his psychological health, for example? We cannot provide clear answers to the many questions of this kind that are suggested by this difference between Town and City in perception of and response to the characteristics of their work, but they will underlie our attempt in the following chapter to interpret these and other findings. Furthermore, these questions about "distortion" by City workers may well add to the concern already expressed when examining individual characteristics, as to the long-run dangers inherent in the City type of "adjustment" to low rated tasks.

Summary

The central finding reported in this chapter is that the lack of association between task and satisfaction for the total population reported in Chapter 3 can be explained by examining separately the response to the task of two subpopulations, 226 who lived and worked in rural or small town locations, and 137 whose "cultural setting" was both urban and predominantly Catholic. Town workers expressed high satisfaction with both job and company when on high scoring tasks; City workers were more satisfied with job, company, union, and foreman when on low scoring tasks. Also, the over-all association between Attendance and the RTA Index (Chapter 2) was not significant for City workers.

The Town-City reversal in response to the task applied in general to the various individual task attributes; it was especially strong in the case of Variety and Interaction. Town workers expressed high satisfaction on jobs with high Object Variety, City workers were much more likely to be satisfied on jobs with low Motor Variety and low Required Interaction, a response that is consistent with the Baldamus' theory that a favorable "working mood" on repetitive work requires infrequent "dis-tractions."

Other important indications that the Town and City categories identified two quite different predispositions or "response sets" in relation to work experience were as follows. The over-all high Union Satisfaction on low scoring tasks turned out to be caused entirely by the City workers' response. The over-all low satisfaction when Pay was in the lowest quartile, on the other hand, was not significant for City workers. Town workers were more satisfied when their age and seniority were high, whereas in City settings high satisfaction was associated with low education and high F-scale scores. For Town workers high pay was associated with high seniority and high education, whereas for City workers high pay was associated with low age and low seniority. Finally, the over-all association between rated and perceived task attributes was much stronger for Town than for City workers. Especially in the case of Perceived Opportunity to Contribute, how Town workers described their jobs was more closely in line with how the researchers had scored them. City workers were more likely to "distort" their perceptions in the sense of seeing more responsibility and contribution potential in low scoring jobs.

CHAPTER 5

The Town-City Difference: Possible Explanations

IN THE PREVIOUS chapter we reported the major "unexpected" finding of this research, namely, that two different patterns of response to task attributes were discovered in our total sample: high job satisfaction with complex (high scoring RTA) work in Town settings and high job satisfaction with simple (low scoring RTA) work in City settings. The purpose of this chapter is to discuss this finding, its possible significance, and how it may be explained. In doing so we will bring in some additional data not yet presented. However, as is often the case, what turned out to be perhaps the most interesting outcome was not hypothesized in the original design. From the beginning we assumed that we might discover different patterns of response to work for various subpopulations, but we did not predict the "subcultural" basis for such differences. Consequently in this chapter we can no longer limit ourselves to a straightforward presentation of findings, but must begin more speculatively to discuss their meaning. We will be raising some questions for which we have no clear answers; we will be turning more frequently to the research and theory of others in searching for explanations for what we found; and we will be implying some relevant directions for further research and experimentation which will be made more explicit in Chapter 6 when we summarize implications from the total study.

To set the stage for the following discussion, it is helpful to review briefly the major difference in the response and be-

havior of the Town and City subpopulations. Workers in
Town settings, almost without exception, behaved and responded in accordance with the prior hypotheses of the researchers. The Town workers on high RTA Index jobs had
both high Attendance and high Job Satisfaction, and expressed greater satisfaction with both their company and
their union. The older and more senior Town workers
tended to be assigned to higher RTA jobs, and they were
both better satisfied and better paid. Town workers perceived the attributes of their tasks in much the same way as
the researchers, and they especially saw high opportunities to
contribute on high RTA jobs. Pay in the lowest quartile was
associated with dissatisfaction, but at higher levels Pay had
no discernible effect on Job Satisfaction.

These "expected" findings for Town workers stand in
sharp contrast to the findings for City workers. City workers
found higher Job Satisfaction on low RTA jobs. For City
workers there was no significant relation between Attendance
and task attributes. They also expressed higher satisfaction
with their company, their union, and their foreman when
they were working on low RTA jobs. The older and more
senior men among them were not more satisfied and were
significantly lower paid than the younger, junior men. Many
City workers perceived high opportunities to contribute on
low scoring jobs. And we have not been able, as yet, to find
any meaningful relation between their pay level and their
level of Job Satisfaction.

How can we account for these differences? The remainder
of this chapter will be concerned primarily with this question. We will not expect to find any final answers but will
be seeking to fit the evidence of this study into a more general
theoretical explanation.

Before proceeding with the discussion, an obvious but important point should be made about satisfaction as a response
to work. Any person's level of satisfaction with a particular
circumstance depends not only on the rewards available to

him in that situation, but also on his needs and wants. Or, as Nancy Morse puts it, "The greater the amount the individual gets, the greater his satisfaction and, at the same time, the more the individual still desires, the less his satisfaction." [1] This formulation serves as a useful reminder that the Town-City difference in satisfaction with the same kind of job attributes implies a difference in what is wanted or expected at work. Unless we understand this difference in wants or expectations, we cannot understand the difference in response. This is why we have sometimes referred to the variation in response between Town and City settings as a difference in "motivational predispositions." Now we need to consider in more detail these two different patterns of expectation or predisposition toward the job, where they may come from, how they may be explained, and the extent to which they may be subject to change.

Town Predispositions

The positive relationship for Town workers between task attribute scores and Job Satisfaction indicates that what they wanted out of their job experience was a relatively large amount of variety, autonomy, interaction, skill, and responsibility. Put in other terms, they were seeking a work environment in which they were expected or permitted a relatively rich and varied behavioral pattern in terms of activities, interactions, and mental states. Apparently they were predisposed to respond favorably to a relatively "challenging" or "involving" work environment, in which more of their potential ways of behaving could be constructively engaged with the task.

It can be seen that statements like those in the preceding paragraph are consistent with a widely held set of assumptions about the relationship between needs and behavior. Under this mode of theorizing about motivation, it is as-

[1] Morse (1953), p. 23. See especially the discussion of this point by Homans (1961), pp. 265–282.

sumed that men will seek out and feel rewarded by situations in which there is a challenge or opportunity to engage more of their ability to enrich their experience, to explore and achieve more varied relationships with their environment.

A number of theories of motivation, differing from one another in important respects, share in common this emphasis. For example, White, in developing his theory of "effectance motivation," has described a persistent human need to attain increasing levels of competence in exploring and dealing with the environment.[2] Other writers stress the idea of the individual's need to develop and grow, to achieve the potentials in himself of which his previous experience has taught him to be aware. Thus, according to Combs and Snygg: "Man . . . is an insatiably striving organism forever seeking the maintenance and enhancement of the self. From birth to death he is continually engaged in the search for greater feelings of adequacy." [3] Perhaps the leading exponent of this point of view is Gordon Allport, with his stress on the "proactive" nature of man, his concept of "functionally autonomous" motives, and his view of personality as "a wide open system seeking progressively new levels of order and transaction." [4]

While the theories just cited differ from one another in many important ways, they, as is true of many others that could be added, have in common that they could without difficulty be used to "explain" the response to task attributes we discovered in Town settings. The greater the requirement and opportunity inherent in the job for the Town worker to exercise increasing competence, to enhance his concept of himself as an adequate person, to attain new levels of order and transaction with his environment, the more favor-

[2] White (1959). A useful discussion of motivational theories of White and others is provided by Gellerman (1963).

[3] Combs and Snygg (1959), p. 54.

[4] Allport (1960), p. 51. See also Allport (1955) and (1961), pp. 212–257.

able his response to the job should be, according to theories of this kind.

An opportunity to explain in more specific terms our data in terms of this way of thinking about motivation is offered by the "need hierarchy" of Maslow (1954). In his theory, Maslow postulates that man is a wanting creature who will under all circumstances be seeking to achieve certain goals, but that these goals will change as he satiates some needs and turns his attention to others. Maslow has worked out a hierarchy of needs that he believes man follows in general terms, being "concerned at the outset" in physiological gratifications, and, as these are partially filled, moving his seeking attention in sequence to "safety" needs, "social" needs, "ego" needs, and "self-actualization" needs. McGregor has written of the relevance of Maslow's theory to industrial settings and has shown how management beliefs and practices can be built upon Maslow's conception of motivation.[5] Clark has carried this line of theory one step further by testing it in one industrial organization.[6] He found some evidence supporting the hypothesis that certain specified combinations of industrial conditions (job security, work group characteristics, supervisory style, company support, and task attributes) induced seeking, concerned behavior in workers that would support the need hierarchy theory.

Following Maslow, McGregor, and Clark, we would predict that a certain minimal level of pay and job security would be a preoccupation of industrial workers until their basic physiological and safety needs were met. Then we would predict a preoccupation with social needs — the need to be liked and enjoy friendly associations at work. As this need became at least partially satisfied at work, the theory would predict a growing concern with accomplishments that would bring the respect of others and self-respect to the worker. If the opportunity existed to meet these ego needs

[5] McGregor (1960).
[6] Clark (1962). See also Clark (1960–1961).

by the performance of complex tasks, the theory would predict that these task opportunities would be sought and valued as sources of need gratification.

The record of findings in regard to both Town and City workers can usefully be reviewed with this theory in mind. As reported in the previous chapter, Town workers in the lowest pay quartile were preoccupied with pay to the extent that for them low pay was associated significantly with lower Job Satisfaction. Once this minimal level of pay was achieved, however, it seemed to have no consistent or meaningful relation to variance in Job Satisfaction. This relation between Pay and Job Satisfaction did not hold for City workers. In order to test the need hierarchy against our data, two further analysis steps can be reported. First we took those workers who received pay in the upper three quartiles (on the assumption that for them safety needs would be fairly well satisfied) and examined the relation between Work Group Satisfaction (as a means of fulfilling social needs) and Job Satisfaction. We found that for both Town and City workers in the upper three pay quartiles, the majority who were satisfied with their work group also had a high Job Satisfaction score ($p < .01$ in both subpopulations). Next we took those workers who were not only in the upper three pay quartiles but also in the upper three quartiles in Work Group Satisfaction, and investigated how for them Job Satisfaction was associated with the RTA Index. For these men, who were presumably meeting both their minimal pay and work group satisfaction needs, we found the now familiar pattern: high satisfaction with high RTA for Town workers, and high satisfaction with low RTA for City workers ($p < .05$ in both cases).

The need hierarchy theory fits quite well the response of Town workers: when their pay was unusually low they tended to be dissatisfied; when satisfied with pay, they responded favorably to a congenial work group; when satisfied with their work group they responded favorably to the challenge of a relatively complex task. But this explanation, as with the other "striving" type theories we examined briefly, fails as an explanation of the City response. City workers did not necessarily express dissatisfaction with unusually low pay. Whether pay was high or low they tended to express high Job Satisfaction when satisfied with their work group. And regardless of either pay or Work Group Satisfaction, they were likely to be more satisfied with more simple, less demanding jobs. In short, the various "striving" theories of motivation are not consistent with our total findings; what is a useful explanation of the City workers' response?

City Predispositions

One plausible explanation of the response of City workers is, quite simply, that they are motivated exactly like Town workers except for a subcultural norm or ground rule against appearing "eager for responsibility." In effect, this idea holds that City workers have been taught by their parents and friends that to express openly an interest in more complex and responsible work is to expose oneself unnecessarily to disappointment and ridicule. Hence, the norm. In conformance with this norm, they express high satisfaction with low scoring jobs, but are aware, at least dimly, of inner feelings of desire for the more psychologically involving aspects of more complex work irrespective of other extrinsic rewards such as pay.

In order to test the validity of this explanation of the City workers' behavior, the researchers thought of two questions that could be put to our available research data, questions which could be stated so that the resulting findings would or would not give support to this "latency" explanation.

Test One. The latency explanation assumes that the City worker has a norm against "appearing eager" that serves the function of protecting him against the disappointment and ridicule of failing to secure more complex work. To justify and sustain such a norm the City worker would be expected to feel discriminated against in terms of opportunities to secure more complex work relative to Town workers. In our questionnaire we asked a question that provides a fair test of the existence of this feeling of discrimination. The question was designed to measure the degree to which each worker saw opportunities to advance in his job situation (for detail see Question 19, Appendix A). The hypothesis was that if City workers scored lower on this question than Town workers, the latency explanation would be supported. The data indicated that there was no association at all between perceived opportunities to advance and the two subcultures and on this test the latency explanation was not supported.

Test Two. The latency explanation is based on the assumption that City workers employed on low RTA jobs are experiencing more or less of some form of distress even though they tended to express high Job Satisfaction in the questionnaire. Our Psychosomatic Response Index, as a measure of the freedom from nervous strain and tension in connection with work, could be expected to indicate this latent distress on low RTA jobs. Therefore, if City workers on low content jobs scored as low or lower in Psychosomatic Response than Town workers on low scoring jobs, the latency explanation would be supported. Once again the data fail to support this explanation. On jobs in the lowest Requisite Task tertile, 71% of the City workers scored high in their Psychosomatic Response and 68% of the Town workers scored low ($\chi^2 = 5.05$, $p < .02$).

In short, our data indicated that the City response was more than an outward conformity to a subcultural norm. City workers appeared genuinely to find more simple tasks less stress producing and more satisfying than more complex work. A low score on the RTA Index, in other words, was more in line with what they were looking for in work, apparently, and their favorable response to low scoring jobs appeared to be the consequence of a fairly basic predisposition or value position inherent in the City subcultural setting.

One way of describing this kind of underlying difference in orientation is to say that relative to Town workers, City workers would presumably produce low scores in "need for achievement," as conceived and measured by McClelland and his associates.[7] According to McClelland's theory, to the extent that industrial workers have achievement needs, we could expect them to seek progressively more complex tasks as appropriate settings for demonstrating their excellence of performance and their rights to preferred social standing; whereas for workers with low achievement needs, task complexity would be a matter of relative indifference, or even have a negative value if it was seen as interfering with other, more important motivations, such as "need for affiliation."

In order to see whether McClelland's ideas about these inherently different motivational sets do in fact help to explain our Town-City difference, we would have had to obtain need for achievement and need for affiliation scores for the members of our sample.   Unfortunately, we do not have these data.   The only personality measure that we secured, a modified F-scale score, failed to discriminate in a useful manner, as already reported.   However, a study by Rosen reports findings that are highly relevant in this respect, and reinforce the indications already given that the City response differed from the Town response because of a basically different set of predispositions toward work on the part of the City subpopulation.[8]

Rosen made use of McClelland's method of measuring the strength of an individual's achievement motivation by scoring the achievement themes in the stories he tells in response to ambiguous pictures in a Thematic Apperception Test. This and two other related methods were used by Rosen in a comparative study of the achievement beliefs of several American subcultures. Rosen's study involved 954 subjects in four northeastern states.   The six American subcultures

---

[7] McClelland and others (1953), and McClelland (1961).

[8] Rosen (1959).

studied were Greek, Jewish, Negro, French-Canadian, Italian, and Protestant. The last three of these are uniquely relevant to this study, since of the four companies in City settings three had predominantly French-Canadian work forces and the fourth was predominantly Italian. All of the companies in Town settings employed predominantly Protestant work forces, with the exception of two companies where French-Canadians were in a large majority.

Rosen reports that the average need for achievement score for French-Canadians was 8.82; for Italians, 9.65; and for Protestants, 10.11. When the scores for French-Canadians and Italians were combined, they were found to be significantly lower than the scores for Protestants ($p < .01$). Rosen also secured data on the age at which children were given "independence training" in the home by these subcultures, and the mean age for this was: French-Canadian, 7.99; Italian, 8.03; and Protestant, 6.87. As a third measure Rosen asked his subjects questions designed to elicit their value position as between (1) an activistic or a passivistic orientation, (2) an individualistic or a collectivistic orientation, and (3) a future or a present time orientation. Each response to seven questions that favored activistic, individualistic, and future-oriented values was taken to facilitate achievement and was given a point. The mean scores of French-Canadians on this value index was 3.68; of Italians, 4.17; and of Protestants, 5.16. The score for Protestants was significantly higher than the combined French-Canadian and Italian scores ($p < .001$).

This evidence goes a long way to support the idea that there are some important and not merely superficial differences between the particular subcultures we are concerned with in this study. Rosen, of course, points out that these differences are in the process of change as each of these subcultures is exposed to the shared American culture. Nevertheless, the fact of these cultural differences at this point of time provides additional understanding of why these subcultures respond so differently to industrial work.

We have seen that the Town response to work was more congruent than the City response to the kind of motivational theory which stresses striving as a basic human motive, and that the City response becomes more understandable in terms of McClelland's notion that "need for achievement" is subject to significant variations between one group or culture and another. An alternative way of thinking about motivation can be applied to our data, namely the body of theory that emphasizes not the striving but rather the *exchange* aspects of behavior. In this case we have an approach to the problem of explanation which at first thought seems to fit more closely the City than the Town response.

Exchange Theory as an Explanation

The underlying idea of this body of theorizing about motivation is of course fundamental to much of economics. Men are viewed as always seeking to engage in favorable exchanges with the persons and things in their environment; they are looking for transactions that will be favorable to them in the sense that their "rewards" will be greater than their "costs."

If we are thinking in exchange terms, the question of whether or not we "like or want something" is meaningless unless we add "at what cost to ourselves." City workers may be looking at the nature of their work in these exchange terms. But the question immediately arises, what will these workers treat as the costs and the rewards of their work situation?

Most labor economics is built upon the premise that workers will strive to maximize their economic rewards with the least cost to themselves, in time and mental or physical effort. In terms of the variables of this study, this economic view of motivation assumes that workers are motivated to maximize their pay while minimizing the cost of a psychologically demanding job. We would expect people so motivated to seek situations and to be satisfied with situations where pay is high and task complexity is low, and, conversely,

to avoid and feel dissatisfied with situations where pay is low
and task complexity is high.

To test this theory in concrete terms we chose to define favorable "economic exchange" as a job with Pay in the higher
half of the range and an RTA score in the lowest third of our
sample. We defined an unfavorable economic exchange as a
job with Pay in the lower half of the range and an RTA score
in the highest third. We stated two hypotheses in regard to
these variables:

1. That City workers will seek favorable economic exchanges and avoid unfavorable economic exchanges, compared with Town workers.
2. That City workers finding favorable economic exchanges
   will report higher Job Satisfaction than those experiencing unfavorable economic exchanges and that this difference in Job Satisfaction would not hold for Town
   workers.

Exhibit 5.1 summarizes the findings on this test. The hypothesis is supported in both parts. A majority of the workers with high pay in the lowest Requisite Task tertile are
City workers, and their mean Job Satisfaction score is 5.4
compared with 3.9 for the Town workers in the same situation. Most workers receiving an unfavorable economic exchange, on the other hand, are Town workers with a relatively high Job Satisfaction score (5.0) compared to the 4.4
of the City workers. Apparently, City workers not only have
a significant tendency to seek favorable economic and avoid
unfavorable economic exchanges, as opposed to Town workers, but we find here for the first time a way in which the pay
of City workers has an accountable relationship to Job Satisfaction. It seems that it is not the absolute amount of pay
which influences them, but its relation to the "investment" of
coping with a complex task. In this sense, City workers are
responding in accordance with an economic exchange theory
of motivation. Town workers are not.

The "test" we have just applied, however, is of a very nar-

Exhibit 5.1

TEST OF ECONOMIC MOTIVATION FOR TOWN AND CITY WORKERS
(129 Workers)

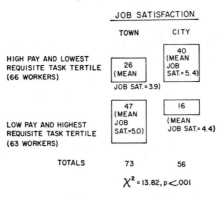

JOB SATISFACTION

	TOWN	CITY
HIGH PAY AND LOWEST REQUISITE TASK TERTILE (66 WORKERS)	26 (MEAN JOB SAT.=3.9)	40 (MEAN JOB SAT.=5.4)
LOW PAY AND HIGHEST REQUISITE TASK TERTILE (63 WORKERS)	47 (MEAN JOB SAT.=5.0)	16 (MEAN JOB SAT.=4.4)
TOTALS	73	56

$$\chi^2 = 13.82, p < .001$$

row view of the exchange process; it sees it primarily in traditional economic terms. In recent years a number of sociologists have greatly expanded the number of commodities relevant to the exchange process beyond the traditional concern of economics with labor, time, money, and tangible goods. In exchange as a social process, other "goods" become equally relevant, such as respect, power, affection, responsibility, knowledge. The literature of this exchange theory has been contributed by writers such as Homans, Blau, Gouldner, and Zaleznik, and has introduced such concepts as "distributive justice." [9]

Under this expanded way of thinking about exchange, the response of Town workers can be explained as well as the City response, by supposing that for Town workers different commodities are relevant to the exchange process. What is a cost to the City worker (investment in a demanding task) may be for the Town worker an important reward (opportunity to express needs for competence and achievement). And what may be a reward for a City worker (for example,

[9] See, for example, Gouldner (1960), Homans (1961), Zaleznik, Christensen, and Roethlisberger (1958), Blau (1955), Blau and Scott (1962).

the "traction" of a low variety, low required interaction job)
can be a cost for a Town worker (monotony).

Conclusion

We have examined two general ways of theorizing about
human motivation to see how they were relevant to the
Town-City difference in response which was the most intriguing emergent finding of this study. Some theories emphasize the purposive, *striving* aspects of personality and seem at
first to point toward useful explanations of Town but not of
City workers. Other theories emphasize the *exchange* aspects
of behavior and seem at first to explain the City but not the
Town response. However, we have also seen that in reality
both Town and City behavior can be discussed under either
group of theories. Whichever vocabulary for discussing the
response is used, the important question is basically the same:
what underlying needs motivate the striving, what kinds of
commodities are seen as relevant to the exchange, and how
are they valued?

The discussion, whichever type of motivation theory is
used, serves the more to emphasize that the difference in response comes about because the two subpopulations in our
sample represent two different systems of beliefs and values
that effect how work experience is perceived and what aspects
of it are felt to be rewarding. These different attitude sets
came to light in our study, we must emphasize, not as individual (F-scale or surname) factors but as social system variables, in the sense that they were associated with the dominant ethnicity and size of the community within which each
plant was found.

This fact tends toward an explanation of the difference in
terms of culturally determined patterns of religious beliefs.
Lenski's (1961) research cited in Chapter 4 [10] amply indicates the extent to which religion influences attitudes toward
many aspects of experience. Furthermore, his finding that

[10] See footnote 1, p. 70.

favorable job attitudes were more frequent among lower class Catholics than among lower class Protestants strengthens the plausibility of explaining the Town-City difference primarily in terms of religious belief. It is undoubtedly true that to a large extent the dominant religion in a particular group does strongly influence the values of individuals at a quite basic level, and thereby influences what they perceive as relevant and rewarding in their work experience. Not only Weber's (1958) theory but also McClelland's (1961) cross-cultural research indicates that task accomplishment at work *is* often (*not* invariably) perceived by the individual as more important to him (i.e., more central to his concept of himself) in predominantly Protestant than in predominantly Catholic cultures.

We should emphasize that the relationship between religious background and attitude toward work is complex. It is not simply an outcome of religious belief in the narrow sense; rather it is presumably part of a whole culturally determined way of thinking that leads to higher value being placed in a given group on certain activities than on others. Weber himself in a paper on "The Protestant Sects (in the United States) and the Spirit of Capitalism," apparently seeking to correct a mistaken interpretation of his earlier essay on the Protestant ethic, emphasized that the influence of religion on work attitudes was not through religious doctrine, as such, but through a religious tendency to place "premiums" on certain kinds of activity, leading to a characteristic "ethos" in a particular society.[11]

In other words, according to Weber's theory, the role of Protestantism in influencing work attitudes was that the religion taught a value system which created conditions favorable to the growth of capitalistic enterprise. It is important to remember, however, that basically Weber's theory is concerned with middle-class values toward thrift and investment. Although he did refer to Protestantism's influence on a ready

[11] Gerth and Mills (1958), pp. 302–322.

supply of "solemn, conscientious, and unusually industrious workmen," [12] his main focus is on the role of the Protestant bourgeois businessman, as far as his thesis on the rise of capitalism is concerned.

Moreover, in our sample the difference we are considering was *not* based simply on religion. We have been talking about a Town-City, not a Protestant-Catholic, difference for a very good reason, as explained at the beginning of Chapter 4. Although it happened that none of our City settings was predominantly Protestant, we did have predominantly Catholic workers in Town settings, and *their* response was a Town, not a "City," response. Ethnic-religious background did not by itself predict the direction of the response to the task. It was important for another reason: in the groups with "mixed" ethnic-religious background, no clear-cut response in either direction was found (and in these groups, as for the total population, religion did not predict response on an individual basis). In other words, ethnic-religious homogeneity, whether "Protestant" or "Catholic," was prerequisite for any clear response to the task in terms of job satisfaction. Given such cultural homogeneity, the direction of the response was determined by whether the plant environment was rural or urban.

Why should a rural or small town environment be associated with a more favorable response to task complexity than an urban or large city environment? Again the relevant question is why in City settings there should be a different set of expectations concerning the rewards attainable from the job. One theoretical approach to this problem is by means of Durkheim's concept of the "anomie" associated with urban life.[13] Under conditions which are more likely to be found in urban than in rural settings, the division of labor, argues Durkheim, becomes associated with a sense of impersonality and alienation from others and from any larger

[12] Weber (1958), p. 177.
[13] Durkheim (1951).

purpose in the task.[14] If this were true, one would expect to find a greater tendency among City workers to avoid the kind of personal involvement with the job which would be necessary in order to experience satisfaction on more demanding tasks. In developing Durkheim's ideas about "Social Structure and Anomie," Merton stresses the importance of levels of aspiration relative to perceived means for reaching them.[15] Under conditions of anomie, Merton argues, people perceive no institutionalized means for achieving the goals which the culture defines as desirable. This suggests that in order to understand the City workers' response we should attempt to measure their level of aspiration, and then estimate the possibility of achieving culturally derived goals within their work experience. The theory would predict that in urban settings the job would be less frequently perceived as a relevant means for achieving the important goals.

Unfortunately our data do not provide a test for the usefulness of this theory in explaining the City workers' response. In fact we discovered no significant tendency for City workers to report less opportunity to advance at work than Town workers. However, this does not deny the general relevance of *anomie* as at least a partial explanation, since we did not attempt to measure levels of aspiration, nor did we discover whether "advancement" on the job has a different meaning for City than for Town workers. This approach should be followed in future research on this subject.

In order to pursue further the Town-City difference in response, motivational predispositions need to be measured more adequately and at a more basic level than we were able to in the present study. Specifically, McClelland's methodology for investigating underlying needs for achievement (and other needs) is perhaps the most relevant in this connection. We have repeatedly been forced to the conclusion that in a somewhat crude way the Town-City dichotomy we discovered

[14] Durkheim (1947).
[15] Merton (1957), pp. 131–194.

in the course of analyzing our data points to some important and relatively deep-seated differences in the perceived salience of task attributes. It seems as if these differences can best be explained by supposing that our City subcultures produce and reinforce an attitude of relative noninvolvement with the job, in which work is not perceived as a relevant means for attaining goals that are central to the individual's way of thinking about himself.

The question of the durability of these attitudes, whether and by what means they might be changed, along with some further suggestions for additional research on this topic, will be considered in the next and final chapter.

CHAPTER 6

Summary and Conclusions

THE PURPOSE of this final chapter is to summarize the major findings of this study and their implications, as we see them, both for those responsible for the design and administration of industrial work and for researchers who wish to explore further the impact of task attributes on workers' attitude and behavior. There is a danger of reading too much into a study of this kind; at the same time our findings do have some important implications for both research and practice which deserve to be stated.

Summary of Findings

The essential findings of the study can be stated very briefly. When attendance records were gathered and questionnaires administered to 470 male blue collar workers across a wide range of technological settings, the results, briefly stated in outline form, were as follows:

1. Perceived task attribute scores were positively related to requisite task attribute scores and to job satisfaction scores for the total population,

    1.1 More strongly for the Town subpopulation,
    1.2 Than for the City subpopulation.

2. Requisite task attribute scores were positively related to available attendance records for the total population,

    2.1 Especially in the case of certain separate attributes (Motor Variety, Required Interaction, Autonomy, Learning Time, Responsibility),
    2.2 Because of the strong relationship between task at-

tributes and attendance records for the Town subpopulation;

2.3 For the City subpopulation, there was no significant relationship.

3. Requisite task attribute scores were *not* significantly
related to job satisfaction scores for the total population.

3.1 Certain separate attributes (Optional Interaction
Off-the-Job, Learning Time, and Time Span of
Discretion) *were* positively related to job satis-
faction measures.

3.2 For the Town subpopulation there was a *positive*
relationship between job satisfaction and task attribute scores (especially Object Variety, Required
Interaction, Optional Interaction Off-the-Job,
Learning Time, Ambiguity of Remedial Action,
and Cycle Time).

3.3 For the City subpopulation there was a negative
relationship between job satisfaction and task attribute scores (especially Motor Variety and Required Interaction).

4. "Situational Factors," some of which might be considered as alternate attitudinal measures of response to task
attributes, did not in general alter the above relationships
between task attributes and response, although the following findings were noted:

4.1 Company Satisfaction and Union Satisfaction were
positively related to task attributes for Town workers and negatively related to task attributes for City
workers; Union Satisfaction was negatively related
to Interaction and Responsibility for the total
population.

4.2 Foreman Satisfaction was negatively related to task
attributes, especially for City workers, and to Variety for the total population.

4.3 Pay was negatively related to Attendance, and
Town workers in the lowest pay quartile tended to
have low Job Satisfaction; Pay had a curvilinear re-

lationship to task attributes (low on medium jobs, high on high and low jobs).

5. Individual background factors did not in general alter the above relationships between task attributes and response, although the following findings were noted:

5.1 Age was positively related to Job Satisfaction for Town (and all) workers, to task attributes for City (and all) workers, and negatively to Pay for City workers.

5.2 Seniority was positively related to Job Satisfaction for Town workers, to task attributes for all workers, to Pay for Town workers, and negatively to Pay for City workers.

5.3 Education was negatively related to Job Satisfaction for City workers, positively to task attributes for Town and City workers, and positively to Pay for Town (and all) workers.

5.4 F-scale scores were positively related to Job Satisfaction for City (and all) workers and to Pay for Town workers.

The above outline summarizes the major findings of this study. Each of these findings implies further research steps that could be taken as well as possible actions by management. What follows is a discussion of the research implications of the various findings that appear most important or interesting to us. Following this discussion we turn our attention to the action implications of this same set of findings.

Perceived and Requisite Task Attributes

The strong relationship between our scores of task attributes and workers' perceptions of the characteristics of their jobs tends to validate the usefulness in future research of similar task attribute rating procedures as measures of job characteristics which are considered relevant by workers who are asked to perform such jobs.

The very strong relationship between workers' perception

of task attributes and their expressed job satisfaction suggests that how workers perceive their task may predict their ultimate satisfaction with the job more accurately than how the job attributes are systematically scored by someone else. However, it should also be noted that this relationship between perceived task attributes and job satisfaction was partly caused by a general tendency in the questionnaire for the responses of a particular worker to various questions to correspond closely. In future research, more can probably be learned about the particular ways in which workers perceive task attributes through relatively unstructured interviewing than through written questionnaires. Whether or not the particular task attribute scales of this study are used in such interviews, the general framework for thinking about task attributes represented by the scales would seem to be useful in future interview studies of workers' attitudes toward the job.

The fact that more City than Town workers disagreed with the researchers' ratings of their jobs again calls for further interview studies of job perceptions across different subcultural settings. This study has raised some challenging questions about this apparent tendency for greater "distortion" of task attributes by City workers, and it seems to us that before too many conclusions as to the practical implications of these differences are reached, considerable further research on the origin of the differences and their true meaning is called for. Better understanding of this question will undoubtedly be obtained through detailed clinical study in particular situations, selected so as to provide various combinations of task attributes and cultural settings.[1] In addition, our findings

[1] The first of what we hope to be a series of such clinical studies making use of our methodology for studying task attributes has been conducted by Vaill (1963) who, after assisting in the collection and early analysis of the data reported here, returned to five of the original sites for intensive observation and interviewing. Vaill is preparing a monograph based on this work which throws considerable light on many of the questions raised by the present study.

on the Town-City difference should be checked in further survey research across different cultural groupings. It would seem that one of the more promising methods for attaining more knowledge concerning the origin and nature of these differences would be continued use of measures of motivational predispositions at less conscious or more latent levels as pioneered, for example, by McClelland and his associates.

Task Attributes and Attendance

The clear relationship we discovered between task attributes and attendance seems to call for further research. Future studies of absenteeism should take into account the intrinsic characteristics of the job more systematically than has been done in the past. Relatively high absenteeism can obviously be the outcome of many different factors in addition to task attributes; for example, the degree of required and emergent teamwork on the job, health and outside interests, supervisory practices, the total climate of interpersonal relationships within a given organization, and the degree of interest and involvement in the organization's total task. A comparison of interviews with workers with relatively frequent and infrequent absences might help to discover the weight of these and other influences on attendance in relation to task attributes. Furthermore, such interviews would help us to understand more clearly than do the data we now have the psychological meaning to workers of frequent as compared with infrequent absenteeism. Our evidence suggests that in general good attendance records were not merely the consequence of greater management emphasis on absenteeism in one environment compared with another, but were to a large extent the consequence of greater interest in and involvement with the work itself. However, additional studies are needed to test the extent to which this is true.

In particular, the task-attendance relationship poses some important questions for further investigation by company-based research groups. It is usually not difficult for management to collect relatively accurate records of absenteeism. However, in our experience management often tends to try to relate the frequency of absences to the characteristics of the worker instead of to the characteristics of the work. It appears to us that a plant management concerned with absenteeism would do well to study the extent to which within a particular plant attendance is related to the nature of work as measured by the task attribute variables we have considered in this study. When such studies confirm our finding that low Attendance is especially likely on jobs with low Autonomy and Motor Variety, management may face a particularly difficult problem. This is so because low autonomy and variety are often characteristic of a situation in which absenteeism is especially disruptive, as on a highly mechanized assembly line.

The emphasis that we have given to attendance underlines an important defect of this study; namely, that we lack other behavioral indices of worker response to the job. We were disappointed with our inability to obtain useful productivity records that could be used in a comparison between different organizations and different technologies. Our studies of the limited records which *were* available to us only increased our awareness of the difficulty of this problem. However, it should be pointed out that from the point of view of company-based research, multiplant organizations that follow uniform methods of collecting absenteeism and productivity data offer an opportunity to study this question more systematically. Especially when there are a number of plants utilizing the same technology, it should be possible to discover whether low absenteeism as a favorable response to more complex work, for example, is or is not strongly related to relatively good performance measured in terms of quantity and quality of output. When such interplant comparisons include both urban and rural settings, useful data will be provided concerning the Town-City difference in response which we found reflected in absenteeism, and, it will be remembered, even more strongly in our job satisfaction scores.

Task Attributes and Job Satisfaction

We have already implied that we believe a considerable amount of additional research is needed before action is taken by management based on our over-all finding on the Town-City difference in response. Even if further research shows such a difference to be widespread, it must be emphasized that our methodology tells little about how inevitable it may be. We do not know the extent to which such predispositions are subject to change, and we cannot even be sure whether they are primarily caused by the difference between Town and City environments with which they were associated for our sample.

On the latter point a desirable research step would be to survey job perceptions and attitudes within the same organization in different cultural settings. If not only the technology but also management policy and behavior can be held relatively constant, the effect of differences in plant location on response to work can be seen more clearly.

On the question of how inevitable or subject to change the Town or City predispositions may be, McClelland's reported success in changing motivational states through intensive training should be noted. But the important question to raise is one on which the methods of this study throw very little light: what is the influence of management's assumptions about workers' motivation in creating or reinforcing a particular response to the nature of the job? What happens in a City setting with complex work when management consistently acts on the assumption that workers will respond in a Town manner, and vice versa? It may well be that here, as in other areas, what management assumes, if consistently acted on, can, over time, create the kind of response that reinforces the original assumption. However, additional clinical studies of carefully selected situations would seem to be the next step in attempting to answer this question.

Situational Factors

Our findings on Union Satisfaction should not be over-emphasized. Our measure of this variable was based only on one question in the questionnaire, "Do you feel that your union is helpful to its members?" The most favorable of the five available answers to this question ("Yes, the union is very helpful") was chosen by more than half of the workers who answered the question. Furthermore, the nature of our sample was such that the answers to this question are probably not representative of attitudes of union members in general. Nevertheless, the fact that union attitudes were related to task attributes in much the same way as company attitudes is worth noting carefully. In recent years a number of friendly critics of the union movement have been stressing the need for official union policy to be more concerned with intrinsic task attributes. For example, our study would support the following comments by Paul Jacobs in an informal discussion with union leaders from the United Auto Workers Union:

> If unions are going to survive and grow in this coming period, they have to break with their old patterns. First of all, they have to break with their pattern of not thinking about work, the nature of work, their relationship to work, and what they can do about work. What do we do about work now? Well, we say we're going to fix the wages, we're going to try to establish what we think ought to be minimal working conditions, we're going to slow down the line, we're going to argue about the speed of the line. But do we ever say: Hey, the whole concept of production of an automobile on a line stinks; the whole thing is wrong; what we ought to be doing is figuring out new ways of looking at the problem of work? No, these are questions from which every union withdraws. . . . I would say that the first step is to stop spending union money on the kind of research on which

union money is spent now, on things like wage problems. It would be a lot wiser for the UAW Research Department to exercise some of its ingenuity and use some of its money to study new ways of collective bargaining and new ways of dealing with the problem of work at the work place, with the union playing the role of the catalytic force.[2]

In short, we believe that unions should be at least as much concerned as managements with further research on response to task attributes.

The relationship of supervisory behavior to workers' response to the task is another area in which our findings point up the need for further research. The fact that City workers on low scoring jobs apparently liked their foreman better than City workers on high scoring jobs suggests that some of their dissatisfaction with high task attributes may be caused by the foreman's behavior. Furthermore, there is little doubt that when the technology requires repetitive and intrinsically dissatisfying work, the foreman who understands his workers' attitudes, who listens to what they like and dislike about the job, and who encourages job rotation and informal ways of increasing job involvement can to a significant extent counteract the negative impact of the technology.[3] There is a need for further clinical studies of the ways in which attitudes toward foremen influence the task response of workers with different underlying "predispositions" toward work. Studies of the influence of foreman behavior on workers' attitudes should consider more systematically the requisite task attributes of each situation that is studied.

The relationship between pay and task attributes was one of the intriguing emergent findings of this study. If verified in future studies, it raises the following questions: Is high pay on low attribute jobs the result of a conscious or unconscious effort to counteract an expected negative response to monotonous and unchallenging work? If so, what are the

[2] Center for the Study of Democratic Institutions (1963), pp. 14–15.

[3] Walker, Guest, and Turner (1956).

long-run consequences on behavior and attitude of this use of relatively high pay and other extrinsic rewards?

Individual Background Factors

Additional research on Town and City predispositions should take into account the different effects of age, seniority, and education, which we discovered in our two subpopulations. Older and more senior Town workers were more likely than older and more senior City workers to be satisfied with their jobs. We have suggested that these results indicate the possibility of serious negative consequences over time of the City type of adaptation to low scoring jobs. Perhaps intrinsic rewards become more important and extrinsic rewards less relevant with increasing age and experience. But this question is complicated, in our sample, by the fact of lower pay for older and more senior City workers. Considerable further research on the interaction among all these variables might help considerably in understanding the meaning and long-run consequences of different ways of responding to the intrinsic task.

Implications for Practice

What are the action implications of this study for the management of industrial work? There are always two dangers in evaluating the practical impact of a study of this kind: the findings may be taken too literally; on the other hand, the findings may not be taken seriously enough. In order to avoid these dangers, perhaps the most useful question for a manager to ask is not "What does this study tell me I should do?" but "What can I learn from this study that will help me in deciding for myself what ought to be done?" We believe that the procedures and findings of this study can indeed help a manager predict some of the human consequences of alternative courses of action, and in this sense help him in deciding what policies to pursue.

The difficulty of specifying the action implications of a

study of this kind is that our findings are based upon the response of workers with various predispositions to a wide range of situations, whereas intelligent action by management necessitates knowledge and understanding in depth of the concrete details of one particular situation. From the point of view of increasing knowledge of organizational behavior in general, it helps to discover that among 470 workers on 47 jobs in 11 organizations the response to various task attributes was as we have described it. But to guide policy and action the need is to know how a particular group of workers, with their own needs and predispositions, will respond to the specific variations in job design and supervisory behavior, for example, that are feasible under circumstances peculiar to that situation.

Our findings cannot answer that question. However, our findings can provide, we believe, more useful ways than existed previously of asking such questions and of attempting to find answers for them. Therefore, our format for discussing the implications of this research will *illustrate* how it could be used in raising and trying to answer questions under certain specified conditions. Since we have been concerned with a *range* of task attributes from "simple" to "complex," and with two different patterns of response (Town and City "predispositions"), we have organized the following discussion under four polar or prototypical sets of circumstances, depending upon whether the technology tends to establish "simple" or "complex" task attributes, and whether the social system or subculture tends to establish a "Town" or a "City" pattern of response. Of course these four sets of circumstances are hypothetical; they are, in a sense, four "ideal types," selected only to help illustrate how under different kinds of actual circumstances, the approach and findings of this study might be utilized. Inevitably also the discussion will bring out how much we do *not* know about questions raised by this approach. Therefore, although what follows is organized around implications for the practitioner, we will simultaneously be repeating some implications for the researcher that have already been presented. To us this overlap between action and research implications is inevitable, since our main research interest in this area is to increase that kind of knowledge which can usefully be applied to the questions which the practitioner should raise.

General Relevance of Attribute Scores

Before taking up the questions raised by this study for managements in each of the four "prototypical" situations just referred to, it is important to re-emphasize the practical consequences for any management of the strong relationships in our total population between requisite and perceived task attributes, and between perceived task attributes and job satisfaction. These findings imply that the task attribute rating scales used in this study, or at least the general way of thinking about job characteristics which these scales represent, should be useful to managers and engineers responsible for the design of new jobs or for the redesign of existing jobs. In particular, these procedures should be practically useful whenever a management wants to experiment with new approaches to job design in which human response to the intrinsic nature of the work is more carefully taken into account. Not only how the job scores on these various attributes but also how workers *perceive* the particular attributes will be highly relevant in predicting worker response to any projected change in job design. During the course of this research, we came into contact with several managers and industrial engineers who were actively experimenting with various ways of "enlarging" the job. We hope that this study not only will encourage such efforts in a general way, but also will provide specific procedures for studying the impact of the relevant job characteristics. Only through continued work of this kind within interested organizations can the usefulness of these procedures be proved and, more importantly, improved.

Town Setting and Simple Technology

When the technology establishes inherently low scoring task attributes, the Town type of predisposition to work will tend to produce an unfavorable response to the job. What can management do about this situation?

One approach to the problem would be to attempt to alter the predisposition, for example, through a hiring policy which selects only workers who do not share the prevailing, more involved attitude toward the characteristics of the work they are asked to perform. There are many obvious difficulties in such a policy. It would take a long time to implement through normal turnover. If a technological change in the direction of more task complexity should occur, the success of such a policy would have most undesirable consequences. And it would result in a working population that might well become more resistant to technological change of any kind; disinvolvement in the task itself probably is associated, over time, with disaffection with wider organizational goals. In short, even if it were possible to change from a Town to a City type of predisposition — which is not at all clear — to do so would contradict a value shared by many managements that workers' experience on the job should be more rather than less meaningful and involving for them.

Nevertheless, for certain jobs, where no change in the direction of greater potential interest seems likely or possible, it will presumably be advisable to try to select those workers who do not object to, or who prefer, simple, less demanding work. In part this will be accomplished by a natural selection process, especially where there is considerable voluntary mobility between jobs. In any case, management needs to be aware of the unintended consequences that may result from any selection policy favoring workers whose values and behavior are noticeably different from the prevailing norms of a particular subcultural setting.

Another approach would be to attempt to compensate for

lack of interest in the job by increasing pay and other extrinsic rewards. In the long run this does not seem likely to succeed in Town settings. Such a policy incurs the risk of arousing attitudes of felt injustice, especially if Town values are prevalent, when work which asks more of the individual (e.g., medium RTA jobs) receives lower pay than work which requires a lower personal investment or opportunity to contribute. Furthermore, such a policy implies that management assumes that workers perceive the task primarily in terms of cost rather than as potentially rewarding for its own sake. A worker with a strong Town predisposition is likely to be insulted by such an assumption. In certain cases it is, of course, necessary to utilize extrinsic rewards in order to induce the performance of inherently unpleasant work. But it appears to us that paying more for intrinsically less rewarding work should only be undertaken as a conscious choice, after weighing the possible long-run consequences against the immediate necessity.

A more promising solution to the problem of simple task attributes in Town settings is to experiment with modifications in the attributes themselves, and in formal role requirements, in order to structure a situation at work which engages more of the potential interest in the task that is characteristic of the Town worker's attitude. More frequently than is usually realized, it is possible in new job designs to increase requisite autonomy and responsibility beyond the levels traditionally assumed by modern work methods study. In the case of existing technologies and jobs, it is also possible to increase variety, for example, by encouraging job rotation. And even within highly automated technologies, many steps can be taken to increase perceived autonomy and responsibility, for example, through encouraging worker decision making on many aspects of quality control, scheduling, etc., as well as on issues not directly related to task attributes such as hours of work and rest pauses.

In short, this study strongly implies that management faced

with Town predispositions and the kind of modern technology usually associated with simple, undemanding work, should recognize that even if the technology requires some low scoring attributes, often other requisite and associated attributes can be changed. We suggest that management experiment, in these cases, with a more discriminating and selective form of job enlargement. Often a careful investigation of a particular situation may show that the particular attributes which are contributing most strongly to workers' dissatisfaction can be considerably "enlarged" without any significant change in the basic technology.

Some of the disappointing results from "job enlargement" to date seem to have been the result of a too indiscriminate application of the concept. For example, a technology that permits little variation or choice in pace of working (e.g., a mechanized assembly line) does *not* necessarily prevent considerable enlargement of autonomy and responsibility in regard to quality or even methods. Sometimes a failure to think separately about the different task attributes has led management to install (without adequate consultation with the workers themselves) dramatic enlargement of some attributes only at the expense of unpopular changes in other attributes that were equally as or more important to the workers involved. The same change that greatly increases variety and responsibility may produce large and very unwelcome decreases in interaction and autonomy. For example, a group of 15 workers on a rotary conveyor are given individual work stations surrounded by high banks of parts, and each is assigned to assemble the total product according to a carefully predetermined method and sequence. This tendency to overemphasize variety and to underemphasize autonomy and optional interaction seems to have characterized several unsuccessful examples of job enlargement that have come to our attention. The worker may perceive his task as a whole, but management, in designing changes, needs to consider separately the different attributes which compose the total task.

The task rating procedures of this study are designed for this purpose, and can be improved as they are further used in this way.

Town Setting and Complex Technology

What important questions are raised for management when the technology requires or permits high scoring task attributes and the predominant worker predisposition is for a favorable response to relatively complex work? In this case, presumably the demands of the technology and the predispositions of the work force are "in line" with each other, and the problem is to preserve and capitalize on the inherently satisfying and productive relationship. It is important to remember that in this situation, more clearly than in any other, *intrinsic* rewards are important. The underlying predisposition implies perceiving the job itself as a potentially rewarding and involving experience; it is important (and also comparatively easy, thanks to the technology) for management also to think of the worker's task in this way, to recognize the value of what the worker can contribute. While this point may seem obvious, all too often management, by misapplying work simplification and standardization to situations of this kind, frustrates not only the logic of the given technology, but the predispositions of the work force as well. The conceptual approach to task attributes we have presented can help management identify this type of situation and thus avoid this kind of mistake.

In addition, of course, management may have the problem of preserving existing task complexity when faced with the necessity for technological change. Some needed changes in process or product may inevitably threaten to decrease some of the high scoring task attributes to which workers are responding favorably. If so, the most important thing to remember may be the importance, to these workers, of perceived autonomy. More clearly than in other situations, undesirable consequences of technological change can be avoided to the extent that these workers actively participate in recognizing the need for change and in planning its impact. They are likely, it would seem, to have both the predisposition and the ability to devise ways of adapting to needed change while preserving existing levels of commitment to the importance of the work itself and of total organizational goals.

City Setting and Simple Technology

The favorable response both of Town workers to complex tasks and of City workers to simple tasks can be interpreted as alternate expressions of the same underlying human tendency to value highly a sense of control and predictability in the environment. To a Town predisposition high perceived responsibility and autonomy imply a sense of predictability and control, whereas to a City predisposition high required interaction and motor variety threaten it. City workers apparently adapt to relatively low scoring task attributes as part of a total work environment which they have learned to expect.

The City type of response to low scoring task attributes underlies the importance of external rewards, and of a feeling of equity in regard to personnel policies as a whole. There is more chance here than in other situations for management to preserve an existing favorable level of morale by means of what Herzberg has called "hygienic factors": security, fair treatment, expeditious handling of grievances, high "consideration" in supervisory behavior, and so forth. A high degree of job involvement is not available and apparently of less importance as a means of encouraging a favorable response. Both management and the worker may have learned to be satisfied with "a fair day's work for a fair day's pay."

Many managers may well feel, however, that this state of affairs is not entirely satisfactory, in fact that it raises some very serious questions for the long run. As was suggested in an earlier chapter, it may be a kind of adaptation that leads over time to strong feelings of frustration at having become so comfortably adapted to a situation in which the work itself is comparatively meaningless to the individual. There may be a danger of creating a working population that is essentially unconcerned with the larger purposes of the organization and that is exceptionally resistant to future needs for change. Managers with these concerns will want, in spite of a presently "favorable" response, to experiment with selective changes in task attributes to determine the extent to which a need to contribute more constructively to the immediate job can be stimulated among workers whose previous experience has taught them not to expect to become very personally involved in the work itself.

City Setting and Complex Technology

If the technology requires task complexity, but the work force is characterized by what we have called "City predisposition," the major question for management is whether such a predisposition is permanent or subject to change over time. The use of the word "predisposition" in this study unfortunately may have a more fundamental and unchanging implication than is warranted. The fact is that on the basis of the present research we do not know how amenable to change the City pattern of response may be. Further research on this subject is needed, especially clinical studies of various groups of City workers *over time,* influenced by different kinds of management practices and supervisory behavior.

Pending further evidence, our tendency is to think of the two patterns of response *not* as though they represented basically different sets of needs, but as alternative ways of attempting to satisfy much the same kinds of underlying needs. We assume that to a large extent workers are or can be *trained* to prefer one of these alternatives to the other, trained by their past and continuing interaction with their total environment, including management and supervision. It is emphatically not a useful assumption to label all "City" workers as incapable of learning a more positive response to task complexity. Such an assumption is dangerously likely to become a self-fulfilling prophecy, since workers are not likely to learn to pay more attention to the intrinsic rewards in the work itself if management believes them incapable of doing so.

In considering the susceptibility to change of City response patterns we should reiterate our belief that these are essentially group or social system phenomena. This suggests that efforts to change the City-type response to complex work, for example, may only succeed if perceived as congruent and not threatening to a wider set of social values and norms in the particular group involved. It is difficult if not impossible to make any general statements about how this might be done, except by means of a sensitive understanding of the total human and social content of the particular situation. One very definite statement *can* be made: this kind of change in predisposition will *not* come about simply by telling individual workers that they ought to have a different attitude toward the job, nor can it be effectively forced by external pressure.

In order to stimulate a higher level of job interest and involvement, and consequently a more favorable response to complex work, it is first necessary to assume that the workers involved are capable of such a response. For management and supervisory behavior based on this assumption to be successful requires in addition a high level of ability to understand the complexities of a given human and social situation, and great skill in relating effectively to it.

Especially in relationship to the "City" response, it is important to appreciate the danger of reaching too many hasty conclusions based on the data of this study before additional research has been conducted to test and refine the present findings. However, even with the present limited data, it appears that certain experimental actions might well be taken, especially when there exist methods of investigating the consequences of what is done. For example, the fact that satisfaction appeared to be higher for City as well as for Town workers on jobs with high scores on Time Span of Discretion should be noted. This is another attribute in which changes can be made without necessarily changing the basic technology. It appears to us that many workers in City as well as Town settings are willing and anxious to take a much higher degree of interest in quality questions than is usually assumed by present job-design procedures. In certain situations there may be an opportunity purposefully to increase Time Span of Discretion beyond the existing level, while holding other variables relatively constant, and then to discover whether this increase in responsibility is associated with a more favorable response to the job.

It is important to remember that the negative relationship between task characteristics and Job Satisfaction for City workers was only significant, in a statistical sense, for two of our separate task attributes, Motor Variety and Required Interaction. This seems to confirm the utility of Baldamus' concept of "Traction" in explaining favorable response to relatively repetitive work. The finding suggests that when the nature of the technology requires low scoring task attributes, it is important for the job design and supervisory procedures to avoid interruptions (dis-tractions) if workers are to continue to feel pleasurably pulled along by the rhythm inherent in the activity.

This also serves as a reminder that just because the various task attributes were very closely associated with one another in this study, this does not have to be the case. Many jobs *could* be designed, for example, so as to combine relatively high perceived responsibility and autonomy with low Motor Variety and infrequent interruptions of the "working mood." According to our findings, such a combination might result in a favorable response from workers with *both* kinds of predisposition. It would seem that performing even simple work smoothly and well can be inherently satisfying, especially when there are opportunities for workers to contribute directly to improvements in methods and to solving the design problems associated with product or model changes. It would be a mistake to generalize with confidence about how workers with various predispositions will respond to such combinations of task attributes, but some imaginative experimentation of this kind by management in a particular location might well uncover ways of stimulating a more positive response to work formerly regarded as irritatingly monotonous.

Before closing, let us emphasize that the preceding discussion has presented some *illustrations* of how the findings and approaches of this study could be utilized in certain prototypical situations. In practice, predispositions are not wholly "Town" or "City," and usually the work is not clearly "simple" or "complex." Nevertheless, we hope to have suggested some practical approaches to structuring more positive responses to work under any particular combination of predispositions and task attributes.

Primarily this research argues for greater flexibility, experimentation, and open-mindedness concerning technology and human response to work. Both critics and defenders of modern technology have overgeneralized its human impact because they lacked a practical way to study the specific job characteristics that were relevant. The administration of changing technological settings and the study of the relationships between technology and organizational behavior can both be improved by continued detailed attention to those concrete task attributes that have proved relevant to workers' response.

Finally, this need is clearly becoming increasingly acute with the increasing rate of technological change. Automation apparently has varying effects on the nature of work; sometimes greater task complexity results when a process is automated, and sometimes the work becomes much less demanding and less complex. And the effects of automation on different task attributes may well be in opposite directions — less interaction but more responsibility, for example. Furthermore, whether or not automation exists or is feasible, any technological change may eventually render obsolete associations that are culturally attached to different kinds of work. Often the job label stays the same after a radical change in the nature of the work experience. We need to keep our ideas about work in touch with the reality that is experienced on the job. We need to increase our ability to understand and take into account how human beings do in fact respond to different concrete characteristics of work. Only in this way will we increase our ability to cope realistically with what Mayo called "the seamy side" of technological progress.

Appendices

APPENDIX A

Questionnaire Response Measures

As EXPLAINED in Chapter 1 the researchers used a questionnaire to obtain measurements of the following variables: Job Satisfaction, Psychosomatic Response, Company Satisfaction, Work Group Satisfaction, Union Satisfaction, F-Scale Score, Perceived Task, and Perceived Opportunity to Contribute. The questionnaire that was used is reproduced at the end of this appendix. As can be seen, it included a number of questions of which very little use has been made in this report, although responses to all questions were tabulated and correlated in the early stages of data analysis.

In developing items for the questionnaire, we borrowed liberally from a number of previous attitude surveys, as well as from published and unpublished studies with which we had direct experience. In particular we used, often in modified form, items from published questionnaires by the Survey Research Center of the University of Michigan (for example, Mann and Hoffman, 1960, Appendix E).[1] From sources of this kind we collected a large number of questions which covered the areas in which we were interested. Many of these questions were eliminated because of duplication or lack of clarity, and other questions were written to provide the needed coverage. This process yielded 94 questions which were used in the Pilot Study. Analysis of these results indicated that about 30 of the questions were unnecessary or gave results that were difficult to interpret; these items were dropped, and a number of other questions were reworded as a result of the Pilot Study. The final questionnaire included 42 multiple-choice questions, two "open-ended" questions, and 24 standard F-scale items. The manner in which responses to these questions were

[1] In addition, the first five questions comprising our "job satisfaction index" were taken from a questionnaire developed by R. P. Bullock (1952) of the Ohio State University.

used in obtaining scores for our major response variables is briefly explained below.

All responses were coded 1, 3, 5, 7, or 9, from least to most "favorable" of the five available alternate choices, or 1, 3, 7, and 9 when there were only four alternative choices. The scores from the individual questions were combined into scores for the major response variables as follows. (A detailed analysis of the pilot study data was useful in constructing these indices.)

Variable	Combined Scores on These Questions
Job Satisfaction Index	1, 2, 3, 4, 5
Psychosomatic Response	41, 42, 43
Company Satisfaction	6, 7, 8, 9
Work Group Satisfaction	34, 36, 37, 38, 39
Union Satisfaction	11
Perceived Opportunity to Contribute	17, 19, 32
F-Scale Score	1–24, "Personal Opinion Survey"

The above indices were constructed simply by summing the scores on the indicated questions. The Perceived Task Index was constructed in a more complicated way in order to use all the relevant questions, combined in such a way that each major perceived attribute received approximately equal weight. The scores for the following perceived task attributes were summed:

Perceived Variety	$= 2 \times$ question 26
Perceived Autonomy	$=$ question 22 $+$ question 24
Perceived Interaction	$= 2 \times$ question 28
Perceived Knowledge and Skill	$=$ question 25
Perceived Responsibility	$=$ (question 17 $+$ question 21 $+$ question 30) $\div$ 3
Perceived Task Index	$=$ Total of above

In general, average raw scores were used in the initial correlation analysis, and in most cases these were converted to octile scores for the purpose of making the cross-tabulations for the contingency tables we have used in this report.

The questionnaire was administered to small groups of workers at times and places (in the plant) convenient for them, which provided an opportunity to explain verbally its purpose and how it was going to be used. A French translation was used for French-speaking respondents. In general the questionnaire seemed to be well understood and the reaction to it was favorable. The questions which produced the most dubious results were those which were intended to assess the relative importance, or salience, for the worker, of the various perceived task attributes. ("Is your answer to the previous question a reason for liking or disliking your job?" — questions 18, 20, 23, 27, 29, 31, 33.) Apparently many respondents did not interpret the meaning of these questions as intended; for example, workers with high job satisfaction usually indicated that each of the different job attributes, whether they perceived them as scoring high or low, were equally strong reasons for liking their job. The responses to these questions have not been used in the present report. The distribution of responses to several other questions indicated that they had failed to discriminate the attitude they were intended to reveal, for example 10 (perceived usefulness of the product), 16 (closeness of supervision), 35 (size of work group), 40 (how hard you work). With these exceptions, the researchers believed that the questionnaire was successful in accomplishing its purpose.

JOB ATTITUDE STUDY

Division of Research, Harvard Business School

This is a questionnaire about your job and your attitude toward it. There are no right and wrong answers. Every individual finds in his job some things he likes and some things he dislikes, and this varies from individual to individual. As previously announced, no one outside the Harvard research group will see your answers to these questions. Your answers will be combined with the answers of everyone else taking this questionnaire, and only the over-all statistical results will be reported. For your answers to be useful to us, it is necessary for us to know your name, although no names or other means of personal identification will be used by us in reporting the results of this study.

a. Please write your name here:

_____

      (first name)   (last name)

b. Please write here the title of your "regular" job, that is to say, the job at which you work most of the time.

_____

c. Please check the highest level of education you have had.
    _____Some grammar school.
    _____Completed grammar school (grade 8).
    _____Some high school or equivalent.
    _____Completed high school or equivalent.
    _____Some college or equivalent.

A. *General Job Attitude*

(The purpose of the first group of questions is to indicate to us your over-all attitude towards your job with this company.)

1. Place a check mark in front of the statement which best tells how good a job you have.
    _____The job is an excellent one, very much above the average.
    _____The job is a fairly good one.
    _____The job is only average.
    _____The job is not as good as average in this kind of work.
    _____The job is a very poor one, very much below the average.

2. Place a check mark in front of the statement which best describes your feelings about your job.

_____I am very satisfied and happy on this job.

_____I am fairly well satisfied on this job.

_____I am neither satisfied nor dissatisfied — it is just average.

_____I am a little dissatisfied on this job.

_____I am very dissatisfied and unhappy on this job.

3. Check one of the following statements to show how much of the time you are satisfied with your job.

_____Most of the time.

_____A good deal of the time.

_____About half of the time.

_____Occasionally.

_____Seldom.

4. Check one of the following statements which best tells how you feel *about changing your job.*

_____I would quit this job at once if I had anything else to do.

_____I would take almost any other job in which I could earn as much as I am earning here.

_____This job is as good as the average and I would just as soon have it as any other job but would do so if I could make more money.

_____I am not eager to change jobs but would do so if I could make more money.

_____I do not want to change jobs even for more money because this is a good one.

5. On the line below, place a check mark to show how well satisfied you are with this job. You may place your mark anywhere on the line either above one of the statements or between them.

I_____I_____I_____I_____I

| Completely dissatisfied | More dissatisfied than satisfied | About half and half | More satisfied than dissatisfied | Completely satisfied |

B. *The Company*

(On all the following questions, please check the one answer which corresponds most closely with your own attitude.)

6. How do you feel about the progress you have made in the company up to now?

_____Very dissatisfied.
_____Fairly dissatisfied.
_____Neither satisfied nor dissatisfied.
_____Fairly satisfied.
_____Very satisfied.

7. Do you think that this company is fair to its employees or not?
_____Very fair to the employees.
_____Reasonably fair to the employees.
_____About equally fair and unfair to the employees.
_____Somewhat unfair to the employees.
_____Very unfair to the employees.

8. How well do you feel the top management of the company understands the problems that the employees have?
_____Top management of the company has *no understanding* of our problems.
_____Top management has *little understanding* of our problems.
_____Top management has *some understanding* of our problems.
_____Top management has *considerable understanding* of our problems.
_____Top management has *complete understanding* of our problems.

9. How would you feel about quitting your present job, if you were offered the same job with the same pay and seniority in another company?
_____Very reluctant to quit.
_____Reluctant to quit.
_____Indifferent.
_____Glad to quit.
_____Very glad to quit.

10. What do you think of the product and services produced by your company?
_____Quite undesirable or useless product.
_____Fairly undesirable or useless product.
_____Average product — indifferent.
_____Fairly desirable and useful product.
_____Very desirable and useful product.

(Skip the following question if there is no union in your plant.)

11. Do you feel that your union is helpful to its members?

_____Yes, the union is very helpful.

_____Fairly helpful.

_____Sometimes it is helpful, but not as much as it might be.

_____Mostly not helpful.

_____No, the union is not at all helpful to its members.

C. *Supervision*

(Your answers to the following group of questions will help us find out how people's attitudes towards their foremen or immediate supervisors are related to the kind of work they do and other aspects of the job.)

12. How well do you think your foreman knows the technical side of his job (the planning, the work, the operations and maintenance of the equipment for which he is responsible, etc.)?

_____He knows the technical parts of his job extremely well.

_____Very well.

_____Fairly well.

_____Some well and others not so well.

_____Does not know the technical parts of his job at all.

13. In your opinion, how well does your foreman get along with his people?

_____He does not get along well at all.

_____Not too well.

_____Fairly well.

_____Very well.

_____He gets along extremely well with his people.

14. In your opinion, how frequently does your foreman stand up or go to bat for his people?

_____Whenever necessary.

_____Often.

_____Sometimes.

_____Seldom.

_____Almost never.

15. To bring all things into consideration, how satisfied are you with your foreman?

_____Not at all satisfied.

_____Not too satisfied.

_____Fairly satisfied.

_____Quite satisfied.

_____Completely satisfied.

16. Does your foreman pay close attention to your work or does he put you on your own?

_____He uses very little supervision; I am definitely on my own.

_____I am pretty much on my own most of the time.

_____Moderately close supervision.

_____Fairly close supervision.

_____He uses very close supervision; he does not put me on my own.

D. *Immediate Job*

(This group of questions has to do with how you feel about your regular job itself, that is to say, the actual work that you do most of the time. The main purpose of these questions is to discover what most people like and don't like about different kinds of work, and how important these various likes and dislikes are.)

17. Some jobs provide a great deal of opportunity to learn more about the work and enable a person to increase his knowledge of the process and his skill; other jobs provide very few such opportunities to learn more. How is it on your job?

_____There are very great opportunities to learn more.

_____There are fairly good opportunities to learn — above average.

_____There is little opportunity to learn.

_____There is almost no opportunity on my job to learn more about the process or to increase my skill.

18. Is your answer to the previous question (No. 17) a reason for liking or disliking the job?

_____It is a strong reason for liking my job.

_____It is a reason for liking my job, but not very important.

_____It is a reason for disliking my job, but not too important.

_____It is a strong reason for disliking my job.

19. Different jobs and types of work vary in how much opportunity they provide a person to advance himself, to get ahead in that line of work, or to be promoted.

_____On my job there is no real chance to get ahead.

_____There is some chance to get ahead on my job, but very little.

_____The chances of getting ahead are above average.

_____On my job there are excellent chances of getting ahead, in comparison with other lines of work.

20. Is your answer to the previous question (No. 19) a reason for liking or disliking your job?

_____It is a strong reason for liking my job.

_____It is a reason for liking my job, but not very important.

_____It is a reason for disliking my job, but not too important.

_____It is a strong reason for disliking my job.

21. In your judgment is the quality of your work the most important consideration or is it of less importance than quantity, speed of working, or other things?

_____Quality is by far the most important consideration on my job.

_____Quality is the most important thing, but quantity or other considerations are important also.

_____Quality is emphasized, but not as much as quantity or other considerations.

_____Quality is given very little importance on my particular job.

22. Check the statement which best describes the kind of job you have.

_____I have no freedom at all to organize my work as I want to.

_____I have little freedom to organize my work as I want to.

_____I am fairly free to organize my work as I want.

_____I am completely free to organize my work as I want.

23. Is your answer to the previous question (No. 22) a reason for liking or disliking your job?

_____It is a strong reason for liking my job.

_____It is a reason for liking my job, but not very important.

_____It is a reason for disliking my job, but not too important.

_____It is a strong reason for disliking my job.

24. Check one of the following items that you think best describes how much of their potential ideas and skills are being used on the job by the people near you working on the same general kind of job as yours.

_____Almost none of what they can offer.

_____About one quarter of what they can offer.

_____About half of what they can offer.

_____About three quarters of what they can offer.

_____Almost all of what they can offer.

25. Please state how much time (in years, weeks, or days) you think it would take the average person to learn to do your job well.

It would take _____

_____

26. Do you have variety on your job (can you do different things, change methods, location, speed of working, and so forth)?
    _____I always do the same thing on my job; there is no variety.
    _____I mostly do the same things, but there is a little variety.
    _____I have to do quite a number of different things on my job.
    _____There is a fair amount of variety.
    _____I have to do a lot of different things on my job; there is a great deal of variety.

27. Is your answer to the previous question (No. 26) a reason for liking or disliking your job?
    _____It is a strong reason for liking my job.
    _____It is a reason for liking my job, but not very important.
    _____It is a reason for disliking my job, but not too important.
    _____It is a strong reason for disliking my job.

28. Jobs are different in the extent to which they allow people to talk with one another while working. Check the statement which best describes your job.
    _____My job does not allow me to talk to other people at all.
    _____My job seldom allows me to talk to other people.
    _____My job often allows me to talk to other people.
    _____My job allows me to talk to other people very often.

29. Is your answer to the previous question (No. 28) a reason for liking or disliking your job?
    _____It is a strong reason for liking my job.
    _____It is a reason for liking my job, but not very important.
    _____It is a reason for disliking my job, but not too important.
    _____It is a strong reason for disliking my job.

30. Is your job something that almost anyone could do, if he had a reasonable amount of time to become familiar with it?
    _____Almost anyone could do my job.
    _____A good many people could do my job.
    _____Only a limited number of people could do my job.
    _____Very few people could do my job.

31. Is your answer to the previous question (No. 30) a reason for liking or disliking your job?
    _____It is a strong reason for liking my job.
    _____It is a reason for liking my job, but not very important.

_____It is a reason for disliking my job, but not too important.

_____It is a strong reason for disliking my job.

32. Does management put emphasis on your doing quality work, or do they emphasize other things such as quantity of output?

_____Management puts heavy emphasis on the quality of my work.

_____Management emphasizes the quality of my work more than they emphasize other things such as quantity.

_____Management emphasizes other things such as quantity more than they do the quality of my work.

_____Management puts almost all the emphasis on things other than the quality of my work.

33. Is your answer to the previous question (No. 32) a reason for liking or disliking your job?

_____It is a strong reason for liking my job.

_____It is a reason for liking my job, but not very important.

_____It is a reason for disliking my job, but not too important.

_____It is a strong reason for disliking my job.

34. Do you feel that people who work with you form a team?

_____Yes, I do feel that people who work with me form a strong team.

_____Yes, there is quite a bit of team spirit.

_____There is some team spirit.

_____There is very little team spirit.

_____No, I do not feel that people who work with me form a team at all.

(Questions 35 through 39 ask you about your "work group." By this we mean those people who usually work near you and on the same kind of job or equipment, and with whom you have an opportunity to talk during the day.)

35. About how many people would you say belong to your "work group"? Please write the approximate number here _____.

36. When you have a problem on your job, how free do you feel to call on others in your work group to help you with it?

_____I don't feel free at all to call on them.

_____I don't feel very free to call on them.

_____I feel fairly free to call on them.

_____I feel quite free to call on them.

_____I feel very free to call on them.

37. How well do the other people in your work group understand the problems you have on your job?

_____They understand the problems I have on my job very well.

_____They understand them quite well.

_____They understand them fairly well.

_____They understand them a little.

_____They do not understand at all the problems I have on my job.

38. If you had the chance to do the *same kind of work,* with the *same pay,* in *another work group,* how would you feel about changing?

_____Very glad to move.

_____Glad to move.

_____Indifferent.

_____Quite unwilling to move.

_____Very unwilling to move.

39. Check the one item that you think best describes the way your group compares with other groups in the way that people stick together and help each other.

_____Much less helpful than other groups.

_____Somewhat less helpful.

_____About the same.

_____Somewhat more helpful.

_____Much more helpful.

40. Check one of the following items that you think best describes how hard you are usually working on your regular job.

_____Not hard at all.

_____Not very hard.

_____Reasonably hard.

_____Very hard.

_____Extremely hard.

41. How often do you feel you would rather stay away from the job than come in?

_____I never feel that way.

_____Very seldom, but have felt that way.

_____Once in a while.

_____Fairly frequently.

_____I feel that way very frequently.

42. How often does your work make you feel jumpy or nervous?
_____Never.
_____Seldom.
_____Occasionally.
_____Fairly often.
_____Very frequently.

43. Check the item below that you think best describes the extent to which you experience such difficulties as headaches, backaches, dizziness, great tiredness, persistent colds, or stomach upsets that you think are mostly caused by your experience at work.
_____Very frequently.
_____Fairly often.
_____Occasionally.
_____Seldom.
_____Never.

44. Summing up how you feel about your job, please list below the four or five things you most like and dislike about it.

The things I dislike most about my job are:

_____

_____

_____

_____

_____

The things I like most about my job are:

_____

_____

_____

_____

_____

E. *Personal Opinion Survey*
The statements on the following pages present various *opinions* about important social questions. Therefore, this is not a test of intelligence or knowledge. We are interested in how much you personally agree or disagree with each statement.

Please indicate your agreement or disagreement with each of the following statements by writing a number from (-3) to $(+3)$ in the space provided according to the following scale:

Disagree strongly	-3	Agree strongly	$+3$
Disagree moderately	-2	Agree moderately	$+2$
Disagree slightly	-1	Agree slightly	$+1$

1. _____Most of our social problems would be solved if we could somehow get rid of the immoral, crooked, and feeble-minded people.

2. _____No weakness or difficulty can hold us back if we have enough will power.

3. _____Young people sometimes get rebellious ideas, but as they grow up, they ought to get over them and settle down.

4. _____If people would talk less and work more, everybody would be better off.

5. _____What the youth needs most is strict discipline, rugged determination, and the will to work and fight for family and country.

6. _____The wild sex life of the old Greeks and Romans was tame compared to some of the goings-on in this country, even in places where people might least expect it.

7. _____When a person has a problem or worry, it is best for him not to think about it, but to keep busy with more cheerful things.

8. _____An insult to our honor should always be punished.

9. _____No sane, normal, decent person could ever think of hurting a close friend or relative.

10. _____Homosexuals are hardly better than criminals and ought to be severely punished.

11. _____Nowadays when so many different kinds of people move around and mix together so much, a person has to protect himself especially carefully against catching an infection or disease from them.

12. _____Most people don't realize how much our lives are controlled by plots hatched in secret places.

13. _____What this country needs most, more than laws and political programs, is a few courageous, tireless, devoted leaders in whom the public can put their faith.

14. _____Some people are born with an urge to jump from high places.

15. _____People can be divided into two distinct classes — the weak and the strong.

16. _____There is hardly anything lower than a person who does not feel a great love, gratitude, and respect for his parents.

17. _____Every person should have complete faith in some supernatural power whose decisions he obeys without question.

18. _____Some day it will probably be shown that astrology can explain a lot of things.

19. _____Familiarity breeds contempt.

20. _____Sex crimes, such as rape and attacks on children, deserve more than mere imprisonment; such criminals ought to be publicly whipped, or worse.

21. _____Obedience and respect for authority are the most important virtues children should learn.

22. _____Nowadays, more and more people are prying into matters that should remain personal and private.

23. _____Science has its place, but there are many important things that can never possibly be understood by the human mind.

24. _____Human nature being what it is, there will always be war and conflict.

APPENDIX B

The Measurement of Task Attributes

IN MEASURING the attributes of tasks that were used in this study to develop the Requisite Task Attribute Index and the Associated Task Attributes, the researchers used the scales reproduced at the end of this appendix. These scales are self explanatory, but brief statements follow on how they were developed, the scoring procedures in the field setting, and what other task attributes were initially measured and dropped.

The Development of the Task Attribute Measurements

Roughly six phases were involved in the development of the task attribute measures.

1. Initially the researchers searched the relevant literature (see references in Chapter 1) and their own experience to develop a comprehensive list of the task attributes that might influence worker behavior. Through a process of logical analysis this list was reviewed to eliminate duplications. The remaining attributes were next defined in operational terms and the initial scales were specified with a range from the least to the greatest quality of the attribute that could conceivably be found in industrial jobs.

2. The preliminary task attribute scales were initially tested by trial scoring of jobs that have been carefully described in the literature. This review process revealed some ambiguities and redundancies in the scales that were eliminated.

3. Using these scales, three researchers independently scored five jobs in a single company. Some problems of interscorer reliability were revealed by this process. The sources of error were ascertained and eliminated by better scale definition or, in some instances, by dropping certain attributes.

4. The revised scales were next used in the pilot study of six jobs in a printing company. Each of these jobs was scored inde-

pendently by at least two researchers. The researchers experienced very few scoring inconsistencies at this stage.

5. A panel of five independent judges were asked to score independently the six printing company jobs from written and oral descriptions of the jobs. This step helped to get the scale definitions into more generally communicable terms and added to the researchers' confidence that the scales could be used consistently.

6. The first ten jobs that were scored in the final sample of 47 were independently scored by at least two researchers to provide further assurance of consistent scoring.

Field Scoring Procedures

All of the jobs in the 47 job sample were scored directly at the scene of the job by one or more members of the three-man field research team. The procedure was to observe the performance of the job for approximately one-half hour and then to interview the immediate supervisor of the job to confirm and add additional information. All of the scales except Learning Time, Time Span of Discretion, and Probability of Serious Error could be initially scored prior to the interviews with the foreman. Some of these scores were confirmed with the foreman on items such as Autonomy, Required Interaction, Optional Interaction, and Ambiguity of Remedial Action. In many instances it was feasible to discuss the various attributes of the job with some of the workers and with an additional supervisor. It was found that the average job could be scored in approximately an hour's time.

Job Attributes Scales Eliminated

The researchers experimented with the measurement of other job attributes that were eventually dropped from the study. These attributes and the reasons for their exclusion are given below:

Requisite Interdependence: A measure of the interdependence between a worker and his work group computed by the ratio between required interactions (I) to the number of people in the face-to-face work group (N) as follows: $\frac{I}{N-1}$. The idea behind this measure was that workers in groups that were highly technically interdependent needed to be distinguished from workers in groups with a small amount of technical interdependence. This distinction would not necessarily be made by the Required Interaction measure alone. This attribute was dropped primarily because of the inability to measure the size of the work group in a systematic or convenient way.

Strategic Position: This was a measure of how strategic the particular job was to the total manufacturing process. Point 1 on the scale was defined as "a work stoppage would have negligible effect on other operations," point 5 as "a work stoppage would have a moderate effect on other operations," and point 9 as "a work stoppage would have a major and unique effect on other operations." The idea for this attribute was derived from Sayles (1958) and was originally conceived as an additional indicator for the Task Identity Index. It was dropped because of the researchers' inability to secure reliability in judging this attribute.

Direction of Interaction: A measure of whether the technology was structured so that the worker initiated task interactions with others or was initiated on. It was measured by the following scale:

Score	1	3	5	7	9	*Blank*
Direction of interaction	Always received	Mostly received	About equally received and initiated	Mostly initiated	Always initiated.	No required interaction.

This scale was dropped for three reasons: because some of the jobs studied involved situations such as assembly lines where some assembly workers in the sample initiated on others and some did not, because of some uncertainty about scoring reliability, and because of the distribution — a very high percentage of the jobs scored as "about equally received and initiated."

Variety of Jobs: A measure of the similarity or dissimilarity of jobs within the working area. The scale ranged from point 1, "all jobs in the area are similar," to point 9, "all jobs are so dissimilar as to make lateral transfers or rotation unrealistic." This attribute drew on an idea of Rice's (1958) that work groups performed better when there was some task differentiation within the work group but not so much as to preclude mobility to more complex tasks. This attribute was dropped because of the difficulty experienced in determining the boundaries of the relevant "working area" for scoring purposes.

REQUISITE TASK ATTRIBUTES

JOB ATTRIBUTE MEASUREMENT SCALES

Object Variety

Score	1	3	5	7	9
No. of different kinds of objects, tools, and controls worked on	1–4	5–12	13–28	29–60	61–120

Motor Variety

	Score	1	3	5	7	9
a)	Change in work pace	Always the same for 95% of the working time.	Midway between scores 1 and 5	More than one work pace, but variations only at long intervals (2 hours)	Midway between scores 5 and 9	Varies considerably during the day. The job does not define the work pace — varies for different operations.
b)	Change in physical location	Sit or stand at the same place for 95% of the working time.		Moves in a fixed work place. Does not have to sit or stand all the time — but fixed working position		Moves most of the time to different working positions. No predetermined position.
c)	Change in required physical operations (as distinct from *a* and *b* above)	Objects and transformation all of the same physical motions.		Some operation differentials but not complex and no important change in process or adjustment for different qualities.		Considerable change in operations requirements.

Autonomy

Score	1	3	5	7	9
a) Method Choice	Detailed and specific methods are predetermined for the job.	Midway between scores 1 and 5	Partly predetermined, but some leeway within a given method.	Midway between scores 5 and 9	Wide latitude given in the selection of work methods.
b) Sequence Choice	Predetermined 90% or more of the time.		Partly predetermined, but considerable leeway in subsequence.		90% of the time the worker sets his own sequence.
c) Pace Choice	Mechanically predetermined 90% of the time.		Mechanically predetermined 40-60% of the time *or* predetermined by another member of a crew.		Can set his own pace at least 90% of the time.
d) Quality of inputs choice	None — completely predetermined.		Some — can occasionally reject substandard material or can reject after discussion with external agent.		Considerable choice in discussing and handling input decisions.
e) Importation of outside services choice	None or almost none.		Has to be discussed with external agent, but initiates discussion and takes part in decision.		Initiates discussion, makes decision and acts, or can veto decision of others.

Required Interaction

	Score	1	3	5	7	9
a)	No. of persons with whom the job requires interaction (at least every two hours) including foreman	0	1–2	3–6	7–14	15 up
b)	Quantity	Up to 5% of working time; short interaction of 10 seconds or less, little talking involved.	5–10% of working time; 10 seconds — 2 minutes interaction, some talking.	10–25% of the time; more than 2 minutes — long periods of interaction.	25–50%	50% up

Interaction Opportunities: On-the-Job

	Score	1	3	5	7	9
a)	No. of people available for interaction at least once an hour on the job (barriers to observe are noise, distance, immobility, mental attention required, and visibility).	0	1	2–3	4–7	8 and up
b)	Quantity (time when one can choose to speak at length to another person while still on the job).	0%	< 0— > 10%	10 > 25%	25 > 50%	50–100%

Interaction Opportunities: Off-the-Job

Score	1	3	5	7	9
Amount of time subject is free to choose to interact by going off the job without reprimand.	0%	< 0 but > 10%	10 — > 25%	25 > 50%	50–100%

Learning Time

Score	1	2	3	4	5	6	7	8	9
Learning (time to be able to master the job).	0 > 1 wk.	1 > 2 wks.	2 > 4 wks.	1 > 2 mos.	2 > 4 mos.	4 > 8 mos.	8 > 16 mos.	16 > 32 mos.	32 mos. up

Responsibility

	Score	1	3	5	7	9
a)	Clarity of remedial action for routine problems	No ambiguity at all. No need for choice and decision making. Not more than one cause for error.	Slight ambiguity. The feedback is not obvious and requires some thinking. The causes for errors are few (1–3) but no problems in deciding among them.	An error can result from a combination of several causes (3–6). Not obvious but can be worked out without too much difficulty.	An error can result from a combination of a number of causes (7 or more). Require considerable decision making to re-adjust.	Very great ambiguity. The relation between causes and effect are extremely hard to identify.

Responsibility (cont'd)

	Score	1	2	3	4	5	6	7	8	9
b)	Time span of discretion.*	0 > ½ days	½ > 1 days	1 > 3 days	3 > 7 days	1 > 2 wks.	2 > 4 wks.	1 > 2 mos.	2 > 4 mos.	4 mos. up
	Score	1		3		5		7		9
c)	Probability of serious error (costing $500 or more to correct, or resulting in serious personal injury).	Negligible.		Midway between 1 and 5		Unlikely but possible.		Midway between 5 and 9	Could easily happen.	

* Maximum length of time before marginal substandard work is detected.

ASSOCIATED TASK ATTRIBUTES

Task Identity

Score	1	3	5	7	9
a) Clarity of cycle or perceived closure.	Negligible sense of beginning or ending in the transformation process.	Midway between 1 and 5	Some noticeable break between beginning and ending in the transformation process.	Midway between 5 and 9	A distinct sense of beginning and ending of transformation process.
b) Visibility of the transformation to the operator.	The operator does not see the transformation he makes or does not see the difference between input and output.		The transformation is partly visible but also partly hidden in the output.		Total visibility of the transformation — output is obviously different from input.
c) Visibility of the transformation in the finished product.	None or negligible.		Can be seen but not obvious and difficult to differentiate.		Clearly visible and easy to differentiate.
d) Magnitude of transformation. (Value added idea. This may be indicated by magnitude of capital investment per worker.)	Negligible.		Moderate.		Considerable.

Cycle Time

Score	1	2	3	4	5	6	7	8	9	Blank
Duration of major job cycle	0 > 1 min.	1 > 3 min.	3 > 7 min.	7 > 15 min.	15 > 30 min.	30 > 60 min.	1 > 2 hr.	2 > 4 hr.	4 > 8 hr.	Unclear Cycle Time

Working Conditions

	Score	1	3	5	7	9
a)	Room	Dirty and dark.		Not too clean, not too well lighted.		Clean and well lighted.
b)	Gas and fumes	Quite a bit.	Midway between 1 and 5	Some.	Midway between 5 and 9	None.
c)	Temperature	Very hot and/or very cold, depending on season.		Some stability, but too hot or too cold.		Stable and sufficiently cool.
d)	Immediate jobs and machine	Dirty, oily, or greasy. Can stain, have to work in overalls or old clothes.		Some dirt and oil, but can manage not to be too dirty with some care.		Very clean and neat.

APPENDIX C

Range and Distribution of Requisite and Associated Task Attributes for the 47 Jobs Studied

IN SPITE OF the fact that the jobs whose attributes were scored in this study were not specifically selected to provide a representative sample of modern industrial work, we did try to obtain a broad range of types of jobs to be found in North American industry. Consequently, the distributions of the various attributes for the 47 jobs studied is of itself a finding of some interest. These distributions, combined with the description of various scales in Appendix B, provide a general view of the characteristics of blue collar work likely to be found in modern industry. Exhibits C–1, C–2, C–3, and C–4 present the distributions for the individual measures and combined indices for requisite activity, interaction, and mental states attributes. Exhibit C–5 presents the distributions for the Associated Task Attributes.

Exhibit C-1

Range and Distribution of Activity Attributes:
Variety Measures

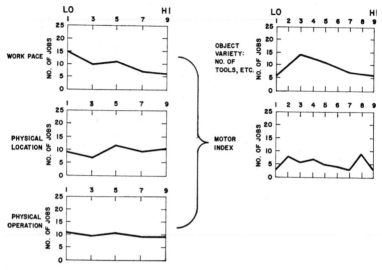

Note: All the Variety measures had relatively "flat" distributions. This is worth noting, particularly in the case of Object Variety, since a geometric progression was used for this scale, ranging from less than 4 to over 60 separate tools, controls, and parts used by the worker in performing his job.

Exhibit C–2

RANGE AND DISTRIBUTION OF ACTIVITY ATTRIBUTES:
AUTONOMY MEASURES

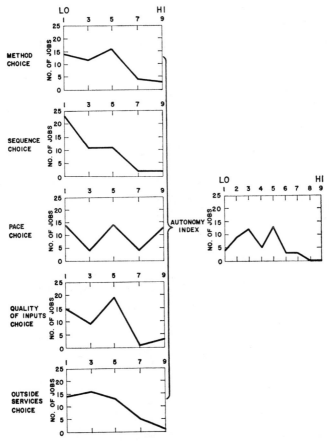

NOTE: With the exception of Pace Choice (autonomy over the pace of working), the various Autonomy measures all fell off sharply as Autonomy increased, in contrast to the flat Variety distributions. This tends to confirm a common assumption about curtailment of freedom of choice in industrial work, but it should also be noted that a few jobs had a great deal of Autonomy.

Exhibit C–3

RANGE AND DISTRIBUTION OF INTERACTION ATTRIBUTES

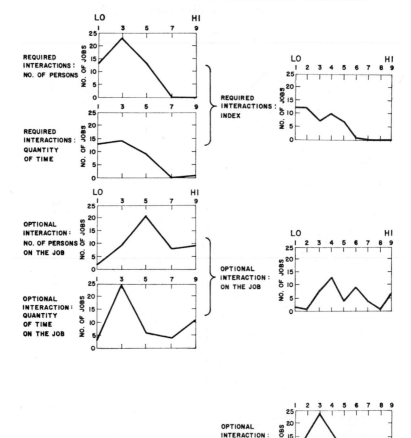

NOTE: There were surprisingly few jobs that required frequent interactions. With only one exception, all the jobs required the worker to interact with no more than six people in any way within a typical two-hour working period and spend no more than 25% of his time in interaction while working. This means that our sample includes few "team" jobs or even jobs that require continuing interaction between pairs, such as between a crane operator and a signaler on the floor. The Optional Interaction attributes show a broader range than the Required Interaction attributes.

Exhibit C–4

RANGE AND DISTRIBUTION OF MENTAL STATES ATTRIBUTES

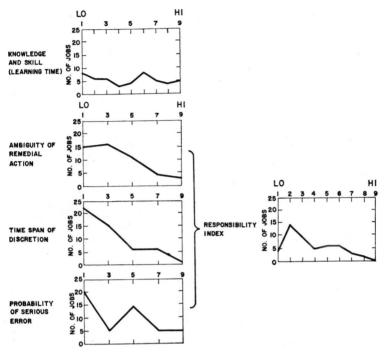

NOTE: The distribution of Knowledge and Skill represents a range from learning time of less than one week to 32 months or more, and the distribution is fairly flat. The range of scores on the Responsibility Index and all three of its indicators shows that a wide diversity of jobs is represented in the sample in regard to this attribute. The distribution slopes off to the right in much the same way as the Autonomy measures. Almost one half of the jobs fell at the lowest step of the Time Span of Discretion distribution (less than one half-day of time discretion).

Exhibit C–5

RANGE AND DISTRIBUTION OF ASSOCIATED TASK ATTRIBUTES

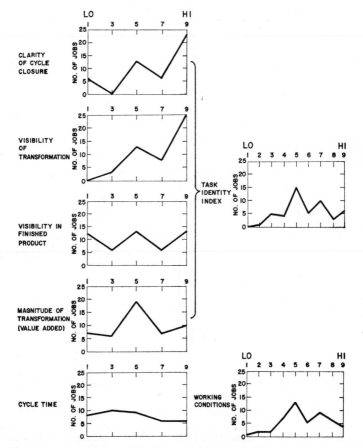

NOTE: An examination of the four components of the Task Identity Index indicates that most of the jobs have a clear-cut cycle closure and a highly visible transformation process. These are the only attribute distributions that peak to the right and indicate that there are few jobs in the sample with a serious task identity problem.

APPENDIX D

Rank Correlations of Requisite and Associated Task Attributes for the 47 Jobs Studied

As REPORTED in Chapter 1, the various Requisite Task Attributes from which the RTA Index was constructed were strongly associated with each other. When the 47 jobs were ranked from highest to lowest on each of the eight principal components of the Index, the Kendall rank correlations, all positive and highly significant, ranged from .26 to .79. The value of each of the rank correlations between the eight attribute measures is given in Exhibit D–1. The rank correlations between the RTA Index itself and each of its major components are given in Exhibit D–2. The correlations between the RTA Index and the five Associated Task Attributes are given in Exhibit D–3. The negative associations with Pay and with Working Conditions run contrary to assumptions often made about how these variables are (or "should be") related to each other.

Exhibit D–1

RANK CORRELATIONS BETWEEN REQUISITE TASK ATTRIBUTES
(All Kendall τ with $p < .002$)

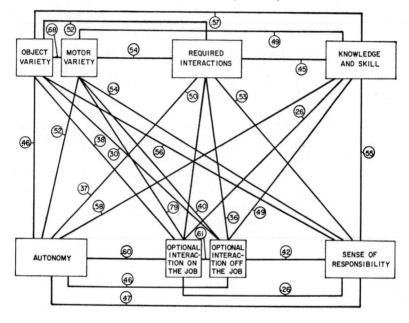

Exhibit D–2

RANK CORRELATIONS BETWEEN SEPARATE REQUISITE
TASK ATTRIBUTES AND THE RTA INDEX
(All Kendall τ with $p < .0001$)

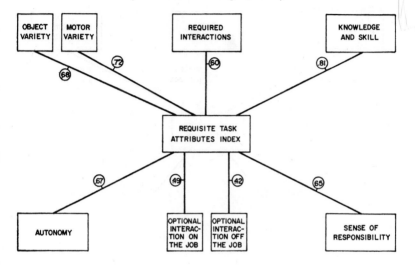

Exhibit D–3

RANK CORRELATIONS BETWEEN RTA INDEX AND
FIVE ASSOCIATED TASK ATTRIBUTES
(Kendall τ)

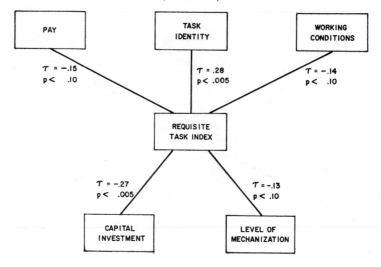

Bibliography

Abruzzi, Adam. *Work, Workers, and Work Measurement.* New York: Columbia University Press, 1956.

Adorno, T. W., and others. *The Authoritarian Personality.* New York: Harper, 1950.

Allport, G. W. *Becoming. Basic Considerations for a Psychology of Personality.* New Haven: Yale University Press, 1955.

Allport, G. W. "The Open System in Personality Theory," *Personality and Social Encounter.* Boston: Beacon Press, 1960, pp. 39–54.

Allport, G. W. *Pattern and Growth in Personality.* New York: Holt, Rinehart and Winston, 1961.

Anderson, Nels. *Work and Leisure.* London: Routledge and Kegan Paul, 1961.

Argyris, Chris. "The Organization: What Makes It Healthy?" *Harvard Business Review,* Vol. 36, No. 6, November–December 1958, pp. 107–117.

Argyris, Chris. "Organizational Effectiveness Under Stress," *Harvard Business Review,* Vol. 38, No. 3, May–June 1960, pp. 137–146.

Argyris, Chris. "Employee Apathy — The House That Management Built?" *Personnel,* Vol. 38, No. 4, July–August 1961, pp. 8–14.

Baldamus, W. "Type of Work and Motivation," *British Journal of Sociology,* Vol. 2, No. 1, March 1951, pp. 44–58.

Baldamus, W. *Efficiency and Effort.* London: Tavistock Publications, 1961.

Bell, Daniel. *Work and Its Discontents.* Boston: Beacon Press, 1956.

Bennett, Edward (editor). *Human Factors in Technology.* New York: McGraw-Hill, 1963.

Bibby, D. L. "An Enlargement of the Job for the Worker," *Proceedings of the 17th Conference, Texas Personnel and Management Associations,* October 20–21, 1955. Austin: University of Texas.

Blau, P. M. *The Dynamics of Bureaucracy.* Chicago: University of Chicago Press, 1955.

Blau, P. M., and W. R. Scott. *Formal Organizations.* San Francisco: Chandler, 1962.

Blauner, Robert. "Work Satisfaction and Industrial Trends in Modern Society," Walter Galenson and S. M. Lipset (editors). *Labor and Trade Unionism.* New York: Wiley, 1960, pp. 339–360.

Blauner, Robert. *Alienation and Freedom: The Factory Worker and His Industry.* Chicago: University of Chicago Press, 1964.

Bright, J. R. *Automation and Management*. Boston: Division of Research, Harvard Business School, 1958 (a).

Bright, J. R. "Does Automation Raise Skill Requirements?" *Harvard Business Review,* Vol. 36, No. 4, July–August 1958 (b), pp. 85–98.

Brown, Wilfred. *Exploration in Management*. New York: Wiley, 1960.

Buckingham, W. J. *Automation: Its Impact on Business and People*. New York: Harper, 1961.

Bullock, R. P. *Social Factors Related to Job Satisfaction: A Technique for the Measurement of Job Satisfaction*. Research Monograph No. 70, Bureau of Business Research, The Ohio State University, 1952.

Burns, Tom, and G. M. Stalker. *The Management of Innovation*. London: Tavistock Publications, 1961.

Center for the Study of Democratic Institutions. "Labor Looks at Labor. Some Members of the United Auto Workers Undertake a Self-Examination." Santa Barbara, California: The Center, 1963.

Chinoy, Eli. "The Traditions of Opportunity and the Aspirations of Automobile Workers," *American Journal of Sociology,* Vol. 57, No. 5, March 1952, pp. 453–459.

Chinoy, Eli. *Automobile Workers and the American Dream*. Garden City, New York: Doubleday, 1955.

Christie, R., and Marie Jahoda (editors). *Studies in the Scope and Method of the Authoritarian Personality*. Glencoe, Illinois: Free Press, 1954.

Clark, J. V. "Motivation in Work Groups: A Tentative View," *Human Organization,* Vol. 19, No. 4, Winter 1960–1961, pp. 199–208.

Clark, J. V. "A Healthy Organization," *California Management Review,* Vol. 4, No. 4, Summer 1962, pp. 16–30.

Combs, A. W. and Donald Snygg. *Individual Behavior. A Perceptual Approach to Behavior*. New York: Harper, 1959.

Cox, David, and K. M. Dyce Sharp. "Research on the Unit of Work," *Occupational Psychology,* Vol. 25, No. 2, April 1951, pp. 90–108.

Cox, David, in collaboration with K. M. Dyce Sharp and D. H. Irvine. *Women's Attitudes to Repetitive Work*. National Institute of Industrial Psychology, Report No. 9, London, 1953.

Dalton, Melville. "Worker Response and Social Background," *Journal of Political Economy,* Vol. 55, No. 4, August 1947, pp. 323–332.

Dalton, Melville. "The Industrial Rate Buster: A Characterization," *Applied Anthropology,* Vol. 7, No. 1, Winter 1948, pp. 5–18.

Davis, L. E. "Job Design and Productivity: A New Approach," *Personnel,* Vol. 33, No. 5, March 1957 (a), pp. 418–430.

Davis, L. E. "Toward a Theory of Job Design," *Journal of Industrial Engineering,* Vol. 8, September–October 1957 (b) , pp. 305+.

Davis, L. E. "The Effects of Automation on Job Design," *Industrial Relations,* Vol. 2, No. 1, October 1962, pp. 53–71.

Davis, L. E., and R. R. Canter. "Job Design," *Journal of Industrial Engineering,* Vol. 6, No. 1, January 1955, pp. 3–6.

Davis, L. E., R. R. Canter, and John Hoffman. "Current Job Design Criteria," *Journal of Industrial Engineering,* Vol. 6, No. 2, March–April 1955, pp. 5+.

Davis, L. E., and Richard Werling. "Job Design Factors," *Occupational Psychology,* Vol. 34, No. 2, April 1960, pp. 109–132.

Durkheim, Emile. *The Division of Labor in Society.* Tr. by G. Simpson, Glencoe, Illinois: The Free Press, 1947.

Durkheim, Emile. *Suicide: A Study in Sociology.* Tr. by J. A. Spalding and G. Simpson. Edited by and Introduction by G. Simpson. Glencoe, Illinois: The Free Press, 1951.

Elliott, J. D. "Increasing Office Productivity Through Job Enlargement," American Management Association, *Office Management Series,* No. 134, 1953, pp. 3–15.

Faunce, W. A. "Automation and the Automobile Worker," *Social Problems,* Vol. 6, No. 1, Summer 1958 (a) , pp. 68–78.

Faunce, W. A. "Automation in the Automobile Industry," *American Sociological Review,* Vol. 23, No. 4, August 1958 (b) , pp. 401–407.

Faunce, W. A. "Social Stratification and Attitude Toward Change in Job Content," *Social Forces,* Vol. 39, December 1960, pp. 140–148.

Fayol, Henri. *General and Industrial Management.* Tr. from French (Dunod, 1908) by C. Storrs. London: Pitman, 1949.

Fiedler, Fred E. *Group Effectiveness Research Laboratory,* Department of Psychology, University of Illinois, May 1963, Technical Report No. 10.

Fleishman, E. A. (editor). *Studies in Personnel and Industrial Psychology.* Homewood, Illinois: Dorsey, 1961.

Fogarty, M. P. *Personality and Group Relations in Industry.* New York: Longmans Green, 1956.

Fox, J. B., and J. F. Scott. *Absenteeism: Management's Problem.* Boston: Division of Research, Harvard Business School, 1943. (reprinted 1957)

Friedmann, Georges. *Industrial Society.* Glencoe, Illinois: Free Press, 1955.

Friedmann, Georges. *Le Travail en Miettes.* Paris: Gallimard, 1956.

Friedmann, Georges. *The Anatomy of Work.* Glencoe, Illinois: Free Press, 1961.

Gellerman, S. W. *Motivation and Productivity.* New York: American Management Association, 1963.

Gerth, H. H. and C. W. Mills (editors). *From Max Weber. Essays in Sociology.* New York: Oxford University Press, 1946. (A Galaxy Book, 1958.)

Gillespie, J. J. *Free Expression in Industry, A Social-Psychological Study of Work and Leisure.* London: Pilot Press, 1948.

Gillespie, J. J. *Dynamic Motion and Time Study.* Brooklyn: Chemical Publishing Co., 1951. (The last chapter of this book was published in *Advanced Management,* Vol. 16, No. 4, April 1951, pp. 4+.)

Gouldner, A. W. "The Norm of Reciprocity: A Preliminary Statement," *American Sociological Review,* Vol. 25, No. 2, April 1960, pp. 161–178.

Great Britain, Industrial Health (Fatigue) Research Board. *Reports.* London: H. M. Stationery Office.

> No. 52, The Comparative Effects of Variety and Uniformity in Work, by S. Wyatt and J. A. Fraser, 1928.
>
> No. 56, The Effects of Monotony in Work, by S. Wyatt and J. A. Fraser, 1929.
>
> No. 77, Fatigue and Boredom in Repetitive Work, by S. Wyatt and J. N. Langdon, 1937.
>
> No. 82, The Machine and the Worker, A Study of Machine-Feeding Processes, by S. Wyatt and J. N. Langdon, 1938.
>
> No. 90, The Incidence of Neurosis Among Factory Workers, by R. Fraser, 1947.
>
> Other relevant reports of the Board are numbers 25 and 26 (1924), 30 and 32 (1925), 69 (1934), and 88 (1945).

Guest, R. H. "Work Careers and Aspirations of Automobile Workers," *American Sociological Review,* Vol. 19, No. 2, April 1954, pp. 155–163.

Guest, R. H. "Men and Machines. An Assembly Line Worker Looks at His Job," *Personnel,* Vol. 31, No. 6, May 1955 (a), pp. 496–503.

Guest, R. H. "A Neglected Factor in Labor Turnover," *Occupational Psychology,* Vol. 29, No. 4, October 1955 (b), pp. 217–231.

Hearnshaw, L. S. "Attitudes to Work," *Occupational Psychology,* Vol. 28, No. 3, July 1954, pp. 129–139.

Herzberg, Frederick, Bernard Mausner, and B. Synderman. *The Motivation to Work.* 2d edition. New York: Wiley, 1959.

Hill, J. M. M., and E. L. Trist. "Industrial Accidents, Sickness, and Other Absences," London: Tavistock Publications, October 1962. (Tavistock Pamphlet No. 4).

Homans, G. C. *The Human Group.* New York: Harcourt, Brace, 1950.

Homans, G. C. *Social Behavior: Its Elementary Forms.* New York: Harcourt, Brace, 1961.

Jaques, Elliott. *Measurement of Responsibility.* London: Tavistock, Publications, 1956.

Jaques, Elliott. *Equitable Payment.* London: Heinemann, 1961.

Jasinski, F. J. "Technological Delimitation of Reciprocal Relationships: A Study of Interaction Patterns in Industry," *Human Organization,* Vol. 15, No. 2, Summer 1956, pp. 24–28.

Kasl, S. V., and J. R. P. French, Jr. "The Effects of Occupational Status on Physical and Mental Health," *Journal of Social Issues,* Vol. 18, No. 3, July 1962, pp. 67–89.

Kennedy, J. E., and H. E. O'Neill. "Job Content and Workers' Opinions," *Journal of Applied Psychology,* Vol. 42, No. 6, 1958, pp. 372–375.

Kerr, Clark, and A. Siegel. "The Inter-industry Propensity to Strike," A. Kornhauser, R. Dubin and A. Ross (editors). *Industrial Conflict.* New York: McGraw-Hill, 1954, pp. 189–212.

Kilbridge, M. D. "Do They All Want Larger Jobs?" *Supervisory Management,* Vol. 6, No. 4, April 1961 (a), pp. 25–28.

Kilbridge, M. D. "Turnover, Absence, and Transfer Rates as Indicators of Employee Dissatisfaction with Repetitive Work," *Industrial and Labor Relations Review,* Vol. 15, No. 1, October 1961 (b), pp. 21–32.

Lenski, Gerhard. *The Religious Factor: A Sociological Study of Religion's Impact on Politics, Economics and Family Life.* Garden City, N. Y.: Doubleday, 1961.

Levenstein, Aaron. *Why People Work: Changing Incentives in a Troubled World.* New York: Crowell-Collier Press, 1962.

Likert, Renis. *New Patterns of Management.* New York: McGraw-Hill, 1961.

McClelland, D. C. *The Achieving Society.* New York: Van Nostrand, 1961.

McClelland, D. C., and others. *The Achievement Motive.* New York: Appleton-Century-Crofts, 1953.

McCormick, E. J. *Human Engineering.* New York: McGraw-Hill, 1957.

McGregor, Douglas. *The Human Side of Enterprise.* New York: McGraw-Hill, 1960.

Mann, F. C., and Howard Baumgartel. *Absences and Employee Attitudes in an Electric Power Company.* Ann Arbor: University of Michigan, 1953.

Mann, F. C., and C. R. Hoffman. *Automation and the Worker:*

A Study of Social Change in Power Plants. New York: Holt, 1960.

Mann, F. C., and L. K. Williams. "Some Effects of the Changing Work Environment in the Office," *Journal of Social Issues,* Vol. 18, No. 3, July 1962, pp. 90–106.

Maslow, A. H. *Motivation and Personality.* New York: Harper, 1954.

Maynard, H. B., G. S. Stegnerten, and J. L. Schwab. *Methods-Time Measurement.* New York: McGraw-Hill, 1948.

Mayo, Elton. *The Human Problems of an Industrial Civilization.* Boston: Division of Research, Harvard Business School, 1946. (First edition, New York: Macmillan, 1933.)

Merton, R. K. *Social Theory and Social Structure.* Revised edition. Glencoe, Illinois: Free Press, 1957.

Metcalf, H. C., and L. Urwick (editors). *Dynamic Administration; The Collected Papers of Mary Parker Follett.* New York: Harper, 1940.

Miller, F. B. "Situational Interaction — A Worthwhile Concept?" *Human Organization.* Vol. 17, No. 4, Winter 1958–1959, pp. 37–47.

Morse, Nancy. *Satisfactions in the White-Collar Job.* Ann Arbor: University of Michigan, 1953.

National Industrial Conference Board. "The Problem of Boredom: Survey of Personnel Problems," *Conference Board Management Record,* Vol. 10, No. 12, December 1948, pp. 567–575.

Naville, Pierre. *L'Automation et le Travail Humain.* Paris: Centre Nationale de la Recherche Scientifique, 1962.

Ohmann, O. A. " 'Skyhooks' (With Special Implications for Monday through Friday)." *Harvard Business Review,* Vol. 33, No. 3, May–June 1955, pp. 33–41.

Picard, Laurent. *The Effects of Personality Determinants on the Relation between Job Content, Satisfaction & Absenteeism.* DBA Thesis, Harvard Business School, 1964.

Purcell, T. V. *The Worker Speaks His Mind on Company and Union.* Cambridge: Harvard University Press, 1953.

Purcell, T. V. *Blue Collar Man. Patterns of Dual Allegiance in Industry.* Cambridge: Harvard University Press, 1960.

Rice, A. K. *Productivity and Social Organization. The Ahmedabad Experiment.* London: Tavistock Publications, 1958.

Rice, A. K. *The Enterprise and Its Environment.* London: Tavistock Publications, 1963.

Richardson, F. L. W., Jr., and C. R. Walker. *Human Relations in an Expanding Company.* New Haven: Labor and Management Center, Yale University, 1948.

Riesman, David, and Warren Bloomberg, Jr. "Work and Leisure:

Fusion or Polarity?" Industrial Relations Research Association, *Research in Industrial Human Relations: A Critical Appraisal.* New York: Harper, 1957, pp. 69–85.

Roethlisberger, F. J. *Management and Morale.* Cambridge: Harvard University Press, 1941.

Roethlisberger, F. J., and W. J. Dickson. *Management and the Worker.* Cambridge: Harvard University Press, 1939.

Rosen, B. C. "Race, Ethnicity, and the Achievement Syndrome," *American Sociological Review,* Vol. 24, No. 1, February 1959, pp. 47–61.

Roy, D. F. "Banana Time: Job Satisfaction and Informal Interaction," *Human Organization,* Vol. 18, No. 4, Winter 1959–1960, pp. 158–168.

Sayles, L. R. "Human Relations and the Organization of Work," *Michigan Business Review,* Vol. 6, No. 6, November 1954, pp. 21–25.

Sayles, L. R. *Behavior of Industrial Work Groups.* New York: Wiley, 1958.

Shultz, G. P., and A. R. Weber. "Technological Change and Industrial Relations," Industrial Relations Research Association (Publication No. 23) *Employment Relations Research.* New York: Harper, 1960, pp. 190–221.

Society for Applied Anthropology. *Man and Automation.* Report of the Proceedings of a Conference Sponsored by the Society for Applied Anthropology at Yale University, December 27–28, 1955. New Haven: The Technology Project, Yale University, 1956.

Strauss, George, and L. R. Sayles. "Technology and Job Satisfaction," *Personnel: The Human Problems of Management.* Englewood Cliffs, N. J.: Prentice-Hall, 1960, pp. 32–55.

Strother, G. B. "Problems in the Development of a Social Science of Organization," in H. J. Leavitt (editor), *The Social Science of Organizations.* Englewood Cliffs, N. J.: Prentice-Hall, 1963, pp. 3–37.

Swados, Harvey. "Work as a Public Issue," *Saturday Review,* December 12, 1959, pp. 13–15, 45.

Tawney, R. H. *Religion and the Rise of Capitalism.* New York: Harcourt, Brace, 1937.

Taylor, Frederick W. *The Principles of Scientific Management.* New York: Harper, 1911.

Tiffin, Joseph, and E. J. McCormick. "Human Engineering and Work Methods," Chapter 16 of *Industrial Psychology,* (4th edition), Englewood Cliffs, N. J.: Prentice Hall, 1958, pp. 460–481.

Trist, E. L., and K. W. Bamforth. "Some Social and Psychological Consequences of the Longwall Method of Coal Getting," *Human Relations,* Vol. 4, No. 1, February 1951, pp. 3–38.

Trist, E. L., G. W. Higgin, H. Murray, and A. B. Pollock. *Organizational Choice: Capabilities of Groups at the Coal Face Under Changing Technologies.* London: Tavistock Publications, 1963.

Turner, A. N. "Management and the Assembly Line," *Harvard Business Review,* Vol. 33, No. 5, September–October 1955 (a), pp. 40–48.

Turner, A. N. "The Older Worker: New Light on Employment and Retirement Problems," *Personnel,* Vol. 32, No. 3, November 1955 (b), pp. 246–257.

Turner, A. N. "Foreman, Job, and Company," *Human Relations,* Vol. 10, No. 2, 1957, pp. 99–112.

Turner, A. N., and A. L. Miclette. "Sources of Satisfaction in Repetitive Work," *Occupational Psychology,* Vol. 36, No. 4, October 1962, pp. 215–231.

Ulrich, D. N., D. R. Booz, and P. R. Lawrence. *Management Behavior and Foreman Attitude: A Case Study.* Boston: Division of Research, Harvard Business School, 1950.

United States Bureau of Labor Statistics. *Studies of Automatic Technology.*

> No. 1, A Case Study of a Company Manufacturing Electronic Equipment, 1955.
>
> No. 2, The Introduction of an Electronic Computer in a Large Insurance Company, 1955.
>
> No. 3, A Case Study of a Large Mechanized Bakery (BLS Report No. 109), 1956.
>
> No. 4, A Case Study of a Modernized Petroleum Refinery (BLS Report No. 120), 1957.
>
> No. 5, A Case Study of an Automatic Airline Reservation System, by Edgar Weinberg (BLS Report No. 137), 1958.

Vaill, P. B. *Attitudes, Behavior & Technical Structure.* DBA Thesis, Harvard Business School, 1963.

Vroom, V. H. *Some Personality Determinants of the Effects of Participation,* Englewood Cliffs, N. J.: Prentice-Hall, 1960.

Walker, C. R. "The Problem of the Repetitive Job," *Harvard Business Review,* Vol. 28, No. 3, May 1950 (a), pp. 54–58.

Walker, C. R. *Steeltown. An Industrial Case History of the Conflict Between Progress and Security.* New York: Harper, 1950 (b).

Walker, C. R. "Adjustment, Individual and Social, to Technological Change," Industrial Relations Research Association, *Industrial Productivity,* 1951, pp. 194–211.

Walker, C. R. "Work Methods, Working Conditions, and Morale," A. Kornhauser, R. Dubin, and A. Ross, (editors). *Industrial Conflict.* New York: McGraw-Hill, 1954, pp. 345–358.

Walker, C. R. *Toward the Automatic Factory.* New Haven: Yale University Press, 1957.

Walker, C. R. *Modern Technology and Civilization; An Introduction to Human Problems in the Machine Age.* New York: McGraw-Hill, 1962.

Walker, C. R., and R. H. Guest. *The Man on the Assembly Line.* Cambridge: Harvard University Press, 1952.

Walker, C. R., R. H. Guest, and A. N. Turner. *The Foreman on the Assembly Line.* Cambridge: Harvard University Press, 1956.

Weber, Max. *The Protestant Ethic and the Spirit of Capitalism.* Tr. by Talcott Parsons. New York: Scribner, 1958.

White, R. W. "Motivation Reconsidered: The Concept of Competence," *Psychological Review,* Vol. 66, No. 5, September 1959, pp. 297–333.

Whyte, W. F. "Who Goes Union and Why," *Personnel Journal,* Vol. 23, No. 6, December 1944, pp. 215–230; also Chapter 15 of *Men at Work,* pp. 268–279.

Whyte, W. F. *Human Relations in the Restaurant Industry.* New York: McGraw-Hill, 1948.

Whyte, W. F. "On Asking Indirect Questions," *Human Organization,* Vol. 15, No. 4, Winter 1957, pp. 21–23.

Whyte, W. F. "Human Relations Reconsidered," W. L. Warner and N. H. Martin (editors). *Industrial Man.* New York: Harper, 1959, pp. 307–322.

Whyte, W. F. *Men at Work.* Homewood, Illinois: Dorsey, 1961.

Whyte, W. F., and others. *Money and Motivation; An Analysis of Incentives in Industry.* New York: Harper, 1955.

Woodward, Joan. *Management and Technology.* (Great Britain, Department of Scientific and Industrial Research. Problems of Progress in Industry, No. 3.) London: H. M. Stationery Office, 1958. 40 pp.

Wyatt, S., and R. Marriott. *A Study of Attitudes to Factory Work.* (Medical Research Council. Special Report Series, No. 292.) London: H. M. Stationery Office, 1956.

Zaleznik, A. *Worker Satisfaction and Development.* Boston: Division of Research, Harvard Business School, 1956.

Zaleznik, A., C. R. Christensen, and F. J. Roethlisberger. *The Motivation, Productivity, and Satisfaction of Workers: A Prediction Study.* Boston: Division of Research, Harvard Business School, 1958.

Zander, Alvin, and Robert Quinn. "The Social Environment and Mental Health; A Review of Past Research at the Institute for Social Research," *Journal of Social Issues,* Vol. 18, No. 3, July 1962, pp. 48–66.

DATE DUE

JUN 5 '91	
BRODART, INC.	Cat. No. 23-221